ENCOURAGEMENT FOR THE ADOPTION AND PARENTING JOURNEY

52 Devotions and a Journal

Rachel Garlinghouse & Madeleine Melcher

ISBN-10: 1507878869
ISBN-13: 978-1507878866
Library of Congress Control Number: 2015902050
CreateSpace Independent Publishing Platform
North Charleston, South Carolina
Create Space, USA

ACKNOWLEDGEMENTS

From Rachel

It's my privilege to dedicate this book to the following people:

My Mom and Dad: Thank you for raising me to know my worth in Jesus, encouraging me to cultivate my talents, and teaching me to live with purpose and passion.

My husband: Thank you for embracing my every creative endeavor with sincerity and pride. Your steadfast love is such an incredible gift.

My babies: You are my inspiration and my heartbeat. I am honored to be the one you call Mom.

My adoption village: Thank you for inspiring, encouraging, and educating me. I would be lost without your humor and wisdom.

My God: You are my confidence, my strength, my peace, and my salvation. I can do all things through You.

From Madeleine

Always for my children, who are my heart and my life. I pray your faith in God and His word takes you through every day on this Earth.

For my parents and all my family who greeted me with open arms and hearts.

For my sweet mommy who gave me my faith, and my husband who shared his faith when mine was weak.

For my sister, Anna, DNA could not have made us closer. XO

For many who God has put in my path who have strengthened me with their wisdom, faith, and example:

For Mary Bryan, a second mother to my mother, whose picture still hangs in the pre-school Sunday school class she dedicated herself to for years. She never married, yet was a mother and a teacher to so many. And for her sweet sister, Emma.

For my grandmothers, great grandmothers and great aunts, who quietly did what had to be done with the strength of a train, and the grace of Southern ladies, and sometimes in the midst of a hurricane.

For Pastor Dave and his wife, Louine: foster parents and parents through adoption who brought my husband to his faith. For Al and Donna, Becky and Todd, Linda and all the amazing parents through adoption I am blessed to know who let His light guide their path.

For Nana Peggy who names us in prayer every day. And for my forever girlfriends who prayed for me and with me on the path to motherhood, and for all my friends who support me now as a mommy. Being a parent is the hardest job in the world and I can use all the help and prayers I can get!

And of course God, to Him goes every bit of glory. It is only by His grace that I have known such amazing love in my life.

PRAISE FOR *ENCOURAGEMENT FOR THE ADOPTION & PARENTING JOURNEY*

"Encouragement for the Adoption and Parenting Journey is a delightful collection of weekly devotions. Quick and easy to read for those who are busy, this book also offers deep and introspective topics that are important to any parent. The questions that follow each devotion are wonderful for a group discussion or for the individual. This is one book that I will keep by my desk, and refer to it each week. Simply a great book for today's parents!"
-Dr. John DeGarmo, adoptive and foster parent, and author of eight parenting books, including *The Foster Parenting Manual: A Practical Guide to Creating a Loving, Safe and Stable Home* and *Keeping Foster Children Safe Online: Positive Strategies to Prevent Cyberbullying, Inappropriate Contact and Other Digital Dangers*

"For me, one of the hardest and most faith-testing parts of adoption is the waiting. Encouragement is something that all moms need but there is an extra layer of complexity and brokenness to coming to motherhood through adoption. I wish I'd have had a devotional/ journal like this when we were in the process of adoption and I'd recommend it to any mom who is just beginning her adoption journey - or any mom who is a mom through adoption. Beautiful, inspiring and healing!"
-Jill Robbins, mom by adoption and birth, and writer of the blog Ripped Jeans and Bifocals

"Oh what a blessing this book will be to those in that painful waiting (to adopt) stage! I would have loved to have found this kind of daily devotional encouragement back when I was first waiting to

adopt. Feeling so alone in those early days I was desperate to find this kind of mentor-ship. To be reminded to lean on God and his word by two women who have traveled the road ahead of you is incredibly encouraging and will bring hope to those in waiting. I highly recommend this devotional for anyone walking their own personal adoption journey."
-Tamara Kielstra, mother by adoption, and author of Adoption Mama Blog

"WOW! This is the devotional & journal that adoptive families have been waiting for! Adoption can test our faith and hope in so many ways. This amazing book will help you before, during, and after your adoption journey. Rachel & Madeleine will reach out and touch your heart with their inspiring, hope-filled, and thought provoking book. This is a MUST HAVE for anyone building their family through adoption."
-Tim Elder, father by adoption and founder of InfantAdoptionGuide.com and AdoptionProfileVideo.com

"A great devotional wherever you find yourself on the adoption journey. Just starting the paperwork, months or years into wait-ing for your first child and losing hope, or up to your ears in dirty diapers and walking on crumbs in your kitchen. Both authors have been there, done that and not only give hope and encouragement to mind, heart, and soul on each and every page, but do so by speak-ing openly from their hearts, sharing their own experiences, and pulling from truths found in Scripture. This book is so accessible and can easily be picked up on a daily basis or also on a drop-in, whenever-you-need-it basis, nor does it require a strict reading from beginning to end. The questions are not too extensive to be intimi-dating, but get right to the heart of the matter and are appropriate

for both individual, reflective study as well as appropriate to stimu-
late good discussion in group settings. Anyone who has walked the
adoption journey will know how your heart is touched and affected
in so many various ways along the path, from the very earliest stages,
in the middle stages of waiting, to the moments when you are driving your long-awaited bundle of joy home. Rachel and Madeleine
have managed to touch on many of the myriad of emotions that the
heart experiences on this crazy, roller coaster ride that is adoption
and they both, in such honest and heartfelt ways that are rooted in
Biblical foundations, give practical solutions, hope, and encouragement to those navigating the twists and turns, ups and downs of the
journey, both on the waiting and the parenting side. I highly recommend this book to any hopeful and current adoptive parent."
-Jessica Schaap, mother by adoption and creator of Domestic
Adoption Support Group (on Facebook)

A NOTE FROM RACHEL

Dear Reader:

I'm Rachel: Christian, wife, mom, former college composition teacher, and writer. I like drinking hot tea, creating art and dancing with my kids, and watching movies with my husband while we eat some of our secret stash of overpriced ice cream.

Our adoption journey began in a hospital room in 2006. After a year and half of illness, I finally had an answer, a "why" to the extensive list of symptoms. My diagnosis was type 1 diabetes, a forever-autoimmune disease that requires 24/7/365 management. I was simultaneously relieved, angry, and hopeful.

As I was curled up in the fetal position on a hospital bed, wearing an oversized gown, with monitors beeping and my fingers and arms throbbing from all the needle insertions, I half-listened to a nurse educator discuss the intricacies of my disease: how to count carbohydrate grams, dose insulin, check my blood sugar, handle having diabetes and the flu at the same time. Then she asked, "Do you two plan on having children?" With this single question, she had my immediate attention.

"Yes," Steve and I answered, without hesitation. She smiled, having successfully wooed me into interaction, and said, "You still can." She went on to talk about what a diabetic's pregnancy might look like.

I stopped listening, because a single word had popped into my mind: adoption.

Since my diagnosis, we have adopted three children. All of our adoptions are open and transracial. Adoption has been the ride of our lives. My heart has been broken and put back together more times than I can count.

I grew up in a Christian home, going to church multiple times a week. My parents ran Bible school and Kids Club, a Christian-based program for children that took place every Wednesday evening. I decided to make a declaration of faith, a decision to follow Christ, when I was nine years old. My faith journey has been steady, but unremarkable. That is, until my faith was tested: when we chose to adopt.

Is God faithful? To whom? What are His plans? What are mine? Do they intersect? Where is my child? Does God endorse or abhor adoption? Should we adopt a child of another race? Where should we adopt from? What about that friend who offered to be a surrogate? Will my husband resent me for not giving birth to his biological children? How do we handle all the questions and concerns coming from our family, friends, and even strangers? Which agency should we use? Can I be a good mom and still manage my disease? Are we really ready to be parents? Is open adoption a good idea? When should we adopt a second time? What if the expectant mother changes her mind after we are matched? What if our children grow up and hate us for adopting them? How do we answer our kids' difficult questions? Should we adopt a child with special needs? What if our family members and friends don't accept our child because we didn't give birth to him? Why, after finally adopting, do I feel so guilty and sad? How is my daughter's birth family doing? Are they healing or hurting or both?

The anxiety, the confusion, the pain, it can be overwhelming and all-consuming. And it can make a person doubt God's love, steadfastness, and peace.

Throughout our eight year adoption journey (and counting), there have been times when all I had left was God. No person, no e-mail from my social worker, no positive affirmation, no glass of wine, no shopping trip could help. Sometimes it was just God and me. Me being crazy-desperate and anxiety-ridden and defeated. God being, well, God. Truth-giving, wisdom-granting, love-bestowing.

I'm not a preacher, a theologian, or even a Bible study group leader. I'm just me, full of contradictions and conflicts, needing grace upon grace every day. I'm a woman who loves God, loves her husband, and loves her kids. I'm desperately clinging to my foundation in a world full of uncertainties and persuasions and distractions. I'm a mom who is teaching her children that God is Truth and relying upon Him is the only thing that works 100% of the time.

Friend, I hope this book pours into your life exactly what you need today, right now. I want you to feel as though you and I are sitting down for a cup of tea at a quaint café and having a heart-to-heart about this adoption and parenting whirlwind (or valley, or mountain...wherever you are at today). I hope this season of your life is enriched by the words Madeleine and I share. And my greatest hope is that this book strengthens your spiritual foundation as you begin or continue your adoption journey.

Let's get into the Word. God won't let you down.
Love & Lots of Sugar,
Rachel

About Rachel

Rachel Garlinghouse is the author of *Come Rain or Come Shine: A White Parent's Guide to Adopting and Parenting Black Children* and *Black Girls Can: An Empowering Story of Yesterdays and Todays.* Her adoption education and experiences have been shared on NPR, MSNBC's Melissa-Harris Perry, Huffington Post Live, The Daily Drum National Radio Show, and in Essence magazine. Rachel's writing on adoption and health has been featured on many websites and in magazines including ABC news, Adoptive Families, My Brown Baby, Babble, Scary Mommy, Rage Against the Minivan, adoption.net, Chocolate Hair /Vanilla Care, Six Until Me, I Am Not the Babysitter, Traded Dreams, Diabetes Health, Slow Mama, Diabetes Sisters, Diabetes Forecast, Multicultural Familia, Portrait of Adoption, and Madame Noire. She taught college composition for eight years before "retiring" to write and raise her babies. Rachel resides in St. Louis with her husband and three children. She blogs about her family's adventures at www.whitesugarbrownsugar.com.

A NOTE FROM MADELEINE

Dear Reader,

I am not a preacher, priest, pastor or church elder. I *AM* an adoptee, mommy to three darlings who came to my heart through adoption, wife to a patriot who gave more than twenty years of his life for our freedoms, and an imperfect child of God. I am a daughter, a grand-daughter, and a sister. My connection to adoption and God's plan be-gan long ago in a car, in another country. I am a Christian, a flawed human being, just working to make my way through the world and hoping to do a little good while I am here.

I am not new to adoption. You see, I was born to a woman with one other child in tow. She was living in a car with the two of us; I was just a baby. After living that way for a time, having little but gas-station food to eat, my birth mother chose at some point to leave me with friends. She did not return. Eventually, her friends had no other choice than to report her absence to the authorities, and I became a foster child. I have no memory of my time with the family that took me in and fostered me. What a true labor of love it is to be a foster parent! I think so much of those who give so freely of themselves to children who need so much love.

My parents were not next on the list to receive a child, yet the gentle faced middle-aged man at the government agency told my mother in his broken English, "I saw her and knew she was for you." At fourteen months old I was delivered to my forever family. I was embraced with a love that held on, never to let go. What an amazing gift! Yet my greatest gift was the faith my mother instilled in me: discovering the love and grace of God.

RACHEL GARLINGHOUSE & MADELEINE MELCHER

Faith. Just a 5 letter word yet it encompasses so much! It has gotten me through the daily trials of life, through poor grades in college, break ups with boyfriends, my mom's cancer and passing, the bumpy road to family building and everything in between. There is no doubt that adoption can test your faith, nearly exhaust your faith and strengthen it all in one day. When we started our first adoption journey (of what would be three), I was worn down by all the questions that it seemed had such open-ended answers. My type A personality struggled with the lack of control I had over much of anything to do with the adoption process. What would I have done without my faith? Where would I be on any given day without God's strength? What kind of mother would I be if I did not work to follow His path and teach my children the same?

Let me be honest with you from the start: I am so imperfect and so unworthy. I actually felt the call to write something about faith and adoption a few years ago but ignored it. I could not believe that God would call me to do this; I am not a first stringer. I have made more mistakes in my life than you could shake a stick at. I don't even want to get into the years of college and my early twenties! I heard the calling and put it on the back burner but I could not escape the feeling that I needed to do this. Me? Me, who has raised her voice, made some really terrible choices, held on to things that I should have handed over to Him, and fought Him at times in my life when He said "no"? I have not been to seminary. I have not ever given any type of sermon. I am not a person that can recite hundreds of scriptures at the drop of a hat. Could He really be calling on me?

Not too long ago I was wondering just that and my thoughts wandered to those Jesus chose to be closest to Him. His disciples. Fishermen. A doubter. A tax collector. The man He knew would betray Him. Jesus CHOSE these people to be his disciples. He did not choose those who always made the best choices or were already strongest in their faith to be his disciples, such as His very own messengers and students. Jesus chose the imperfect. That is a requirement I can fill. A requirement we all can.

So I am here, ready to pour out my heart and share my walk with you: my adoption journey and the part faith, God, and Jesus played in it. Hold my hand. Listen. Share. I will laugh with you and cry with you. We are not perfect and neither is life. God will call on you at some point to be a messenger, a sharer, a teacher. Remember those that have gone before you in their calling. So imperfect, just like us. If we were perfect we wouldn't need Jesus and His sacrifice, and God's great grace. So let's do this! We will just be a big old heap of questions, imperfections, love and understanding. Let Him guide us to all we can be.

With lots of ♥ and every bit of my heart,
Madeleine

About Madeleine

Madeleine Melcher is an adoptee, mommy through adoption, and author of *How to Create a Successful Adoption Portfolio.* She's the owner and creator of Our Journey to You, an adoption profile creation business. Madeleine's adoption story and writing has been showcased on a number of websites, blogs and radio programs, including but not limited to adoption.net, America Adopts, Adoptimist, Mom at Last, Infant Adoption Guide, Creating a Family, My Very Own Blanket, TAFicity, Scary Mommy, and Daily Worth. Madeleine's story and writing were also featured in the acclaimed Portrait of Adoption series (2014). Madeleine's own adoption blog can be found at ourjourney-toyouadoption.com. As an adoptee and parent through adoption, as well as an imperfect child of God, Madeleine has a unique perspective on the role of faith along her adoption journey. She loves life with her husband and her three children and is thankful for all the blessings that have come to her through God and adoption.

HOW TO USE THIS BOOK

We are mothers, wives, and writers, and we know how busy life can get! We don't want to overwhelm you, nor do we wish to interfere with any other Bible reading or Bible studies you are participating in. Rather, we are providing you with a conversational, practical, weekly devotional written specifically for your heart's needs as prospective or current adoptive parent. Our 52 devotions will carry you through an entire year of your journey, and once you are finished, you can start again. The messages and verses we share are timeless!

Here are some ways you may choose to utilize the book:

- Read the devotions in the order presented, or flip to whichever topic is speaking to your heart on any given week.

- Utilize the blank spaces provided to respond to the questions at the end of each devotion or journal on whatever you wish. You can date your responses so you can reflect on your answers at a later date, seeing how you have evolved spiritually as a person, partner, and parent.

- Journal your thoughts, feelings, questions, or letters to your current or future child on the pages provided at the end of the book. You can even doodle, copy favorite verses, song lyrics, or poems, or write prayers.

- Read the book with your partner and use the questions at the end of each devotional as discussion questions.

- Buy a copy for yourself and for a friend or relative who is adopting, is interested in adoption, or who has already adopted. Get together once a week and talk about a chosen devotional.

- Utilize the book in your adoption support group, using it as a springboard for group discussion.

AN INVITATION TO CONNECT

We are honored that you have chosen to read our book! Please connect with us and share how you are being encouraged along your journey. Here's where you can find us:

- Join the book's Facebook page. We will post a weekly topic from the book for our page followers to respond to. This is also a great place to ask us questions, keep up with our latest projects, and enter to win fantastic prizes. Find us at: https://www.facebook.com/adoptiondevotional
- Follow us on Twitter: @whitebrownsugar (Rachel) and @madeleinemelch5 (Madeleine)
- Send us an e-mail: adoptiondevotional@gmail.com

ORDER OF DEVOTIONALS

1

ABUNDANCE

"And he said, 'Bring them here to me.' Then he ordered the crowds
to sit down on the grass, and taking the five loaves and the two
fish, he looked up to heaven and said a blessing. Then he broke the
loaves and gave them to the disciples, and the disciples gave them
to the crowds. And they all ate and were satisfied. And they took up
twelve baskets full of the broken pieces left over."
Matthew 14:18-20

I don't know if you have noticed, but no one ever RSVP's anymore.
If you have not noticed yet, then you will once your kiddos start
inviting friends from school to their birthday parties. This always leaves me in a tough spot when I decide how much food to have
ready and how many little favor bags to make. And it never fails; there
will always be people who arrive to the party without letting me know
they are coming. Sometimes they bring younger siblings. I was no
doubt raised by a Southern lady: I will always welcome another person to the table, I do, however, wish I knew how many I was baking
for! So needless to say, I always keep extra favor bags on hand and
overbuy party food.

I would never want anyone to be left out. I would not want any
child to leave hungry or to leave sad because they did not get a favor.

(Do not think it is lost on me what a first-world problem not getting some candy and a plastic crown is, but when you are five it can feel like the end of the world) I wonder if that is what Jesus felt like when he fed the multitudes with His five loaves and two fish. No doubt He wanted to nourish the souls and the bodies of those that came to His gathering. He cared about all of them. Many of them did not even know Him before they arrived to listen to His words, but they needed him and he was there. He was going to provide for those people whether he had planned to or not. He cared.

In the time of King David, when you went to a party, the fullness of your cup was actually a reflection of if your company was still wanted. If your cup was empty, it was time for you to go. If your cup was full you were welcome to stay. OUR CUPS are "running over" (23rd Psalm). Our basic needs are more than met and God had it all prepared ahead of time for us, His guests. He is truly the most abundant host and will give you what you need today and welcomes you before His throne to pray for any special blessings, as well. I want to remind you that God and Jesus are there for you always, whether you have RSVP'd or not. They are ready to provide for you. They care about your body and your soul. If you have not ever truly known God and Jesus, that is okay. Their door is open. They always have more room at the table and are ready to share an abundance of love with you. They too have an abundance prepared for extra guests.

There are times in life when we recognize the abundance of blessings we are surrounded with, blessings that we sometimes also take for granted: family, a warm home, food in the fridge, electricity, chocolate whenever you might want it, running water. It is easy to forget that abundance when we feel something is lacking. When we have struggled in building a family, feel no control in our next steps or are trying to help a child with physical or emotional issues we do not feel capable of helping with, it is hard to count our blessings. When we are struggling it is harder to see the abundance that God has already provided us. It is harder to see that God's abundant love has remained constant all along.

Feel God's constant abundance for you. Let it not just be on days when your heart is bursting with joy because you have been matched, your child is born, or he or she has reached a milestone. God prepared a place for you, filled it with innumerable blessings, and is overjoyed to see you whether you RSVP'd or not. That is a true abundance.

Even on your worst day of your adoption journey, you have an abundant life and a God who is ready for you, no invitation or RSVP needed. So, if your day feels rough, imagine your overflowing cup, talk to God, and count your blessings. Abundance is here and more awaits.

With ♥ & lots of bread and fish-
Madeleine

What are your greatest blessings?
What is holding you back from seeing your own abundance?
Do you have a harder time recognizing what you DO have because something is truly lacking?

2

ACCEPTANCE

"Not that I am speaking of being in need, for I have learned in whatever situation I am to be content."
Philippians 4:11

I have been in two desperate situations in my life. The first was when I was diagnosed with an autoimmune disease after becoming increasingly ill over a one-and-half-year period. It was a mild day in March when an ER doctor burst into my room and told me I had a forever disease that required 24/7 management. Later, two nurses told me I was lucky to be alive. But I didn't feel lucky. Instead, I was grieving my failing body, and angry that for the rest of my life I would be dealing with needles, carbohydrate counting, and medical appointments.

This desperate situation led to another: adopting. Because my disease can make pregnancy dangerous, and my disease can be passed on to a biological child, we chose to adopt. After finally choosing an agency and completing a home study, we started waiting for our child. For fourteen months, I remember being told over and over "not this time," when we learned that another expectant mother hadn't selected us to parent her child. Meanwhile, my friends were having babies (yes, babies: plural) and other couples adopted. I was rearranging (and rearranging, and rearranging) a nursery that didn't house a baby.

Looking back at my diagnosis (nine years ago) and waiting for our first child (almost eight years ago), I wish I could have looked up rather than down. I spent too many days, weeks, and months relishing in restlessness, confusion, anger, hurt, and jealousy. I found some sort of sick sense of joy in being sad and always searching for something in people and things that always failed to measure up to what I really needed: true contentment and acceptance of today's joys.

There is nothing wrong with being "in need." In fact, Jesus wants to be our all-in-all (Colossians 1:17). He knows we will have troubles. What He wants for us is to learn to be content in all circumstances, not just in the happiest of times. But how is this possible? Doesn't acceptance mean settling for things we do not really desire?

Not at all. Acceptance means trusting that God knows our desires and will care for us. Meanwhile, our job is to be thankful for our daily bread and embrace God's gift of acceptance.

In contentment,
Rachel

What is hindering you from acceptance today?
What is one thing you can lay at God's feet, thus taking a step toward acceptance?

3

CELEBRATION

"a time to weep, and a time to laugh; a time to mourn,
and a time to dance"
Ecclesiastes 3:4

C hoosing to adopt almost always involves some sort of personal
loss: loss of fertility, loss of premature child or a miscarried
child, loss of personal health, loss of a dream or vision for
one's life. Simply put, adoption often begins from a hurting place.
Your path to parenthood may have been quite long and tumultuous.
It may have been months, years, or even a decade's worth of loss, re-
jection, sadness, confusion, and frustration.

But then the day comes, the day you receive the call or e-mail
you've been waiting for. You have been chosen! And once that child
is in your arms, it's time to celebrate! The Bible reminds us that there
is a season for all things and that life is full of ups and downs: seasons.
Celebrations should be included, because a child has joined his or
her forever family, and the trajectory of the family's life has changed
forever.

Celebrating such an occasion is not simply for the benefit of the
family. Commemorating such a life-changing, joy-inducing event is
a way to bring honor and glory to God. Though I do not personally

believe that God desires for a biological parent and child to be separated, I do believe that He can use all circumstances to serve a holy purpose. An adoption, through ethical terms, can be a process, event, and path that demonstrates God's goodness.

Celebrations big and small help us remember how blessed we are as parents, how honored we are to have been chosen, and how incredibly fortunate we are to be called "mom" or "dad." Mark special days on your calendar (the day you found out you were matched with your child, the day you finalized the adoption, etc.) and, with your child's feelings in consideration, celebrate! Make a favorite dinner, put up decorations, wear a new outfit, flip through photo albums, reflect on two cultures merging, create new traditions. And, above all, verbalize your joy and thankfulness to God.

In celebration,
Rachel

What are some ways your family celebrates adoption?
What are some new traditions you can create to rejoice in God's goodness?

4

CHEERFULNESS

"A joyful heart is good medicine, but a crushed
spirit dries up the bones."
Proverbs 17:22

When adopting or facing tough challenges as an adoptive parent, discouragement, frustration, and helplessness can easily creep in. These feelings can take root in our hearts, clouding our ability to have a cheerful attitude and outlook on our path to parenthood and our life in general.

We often do not have a say-so in what happens to us. Inevitably, all adoption and parenting paths have their valleys, some small, some great: valleys we didn't choose or wish for. Sometimes it seems as though we have a mark on our backs and that we will never hear good news. Hearing "no" can be a relentless monster, tearing at our hearts, beckoning us to slip into despair.

When we chose to adopt, we waited fourteen months for our first child. During that time, our profile book was shown about fifteen times to expectant parents who were considering adoption. Four of those times, we were selected as the couple or mother's top choice, and all four times, they chose to parent. Of course, we were feeling desperate and eager to become parents, yet we found peace and joy knowing that the child would remain with his or her biological family.

Choosing cheerfulness is not easy. But the alternative is to choose a "crushed spirit." The latter takes much more work and energy, and it bleeds into every nook and cranny. Conversely, a cheerful heart is healing, it's redemptive, it's simply beautiful. And it rubs off on those around us. Cheerfulness improves our quality of life and makes us better parents or parents-to-be.

There are simply no shortcuts. Choosing to adopt, navigating the journey, and later, parenting children who have been adopted, is hardly a cake-walk. But one way to cope with the inevitable challenges is to choose "good medicine": a cheerful heart.

In cheerfulness,
Rachel

What challenges are you facing today that are leading you to accept a crushed spirit rather than cheerfulness?
What practical steps can you take to help you choose cheerfulness?
What things and people bring you joy?

5

COMMITMENT

"Commit your work to the Lord, and
your plans will be established."
Proverbs 16:3

When you choose to adopt, you quickly get the message: It's all about you.

What I mean is, you are the one who chooses which agency to use, what type of adoption to pursue, how much money you can spend, and, then there is the dreaded checklist. What age of child will you adopt? What race? Will you adopt a child with special needs? Which special needs? Boy or girl? Multiples? What if the biological mother used drugs or alcohol or has a history of mental illness? Which type of adoption—closed, semi-open, or open?

This you-centric philosophy can take root in your heart, and you may begin to feel entitled. The problem, of course, is that the choices you make regarding adoption will ultimately affect the child. The decisions you make change the trajectory of the child's life.

It's essential that as you make decisions before and after adopting, that you "commit your work to the Lord." This means investing time and energy in reading His word, in praying (and in particular, listening to His leading), and in seeking wise counsel from other Christians. Starting with God is a guaranteed win.

The second part of this verse offers an incredible promise. If we commit our lives, our choices, and our "work" to the Lord, our "plans will be established." What we should (and shouldn't do) will be made clear. The word "established" implies certainty and confidence, rather than uncertainty and unrest. We will be able to walk the path laid for us, relishing in God's gifts of peace, grace, love, and joy.

Committed and established,
Rachel

What decisions have you made in what you believed to be your own best interest? How did this choice make you ultimately feel?
In what ways can you commit to God rather than yourself?

6

COMMUNITY

"Finally, all of you, be like-minded, be sympathetic, love one
another, be compassionate and humble."
1 Peter 3:8

Community is a central theme in the Bible. From the beginning, God makes known that He values the coming together of people, starting with Adam and Eve. God didn't want us to journey life alone. Jesus had an entourage-of-sorts: His disciples. The Bible talks about how crowds with gather around and follow Jesus, waiting and watching to see what He might do next. Some may argue that community is a commandment, not a suggestion (Hebrews 10:25).

One Sunday morning, my husband was attempting to leave for church with two of our children while I stayed home with our oldest who had a case of pink eye. After getting the two younger children into our minivan, my husband turned the key to discover the van wouldn't start. Our mischievous middle child had been playing with one of the van's interior lights the day before and had left it on all night. Already running late, my frustrated spouse dug through the garage shelving to find jumper cables. It was an unpleasantly cold winter morning as we maneuvered his SUV nose-to-nose with the van, attached the cables to both vehicle batteries, and got the van running. Our team effort made the job easier, less stressful, and quick. We gave one another a high-five, and he hopped in the van and headed to church.

Adoption and subsequent parenting isn't a journey to be made alone. To cast aside the wisdom of the more experienced or the empathy and support of those who you love you would be foolish. God has blessed individuals with convictions, passions, talents, and gifts in order to bestow those things upon others: to bless, to convince, to encourage.

Though society values independence and a "can do" attitude, God proclaims in Genesis that community, among the other things He created, is "very good" (1:31). Together great feats can be accomplished, great challenges can be overcome, great problems can be solved, and great ideas can be brought to fruition. Within community one receives possibility, hope, and goodness.

In communal hope,
Rachel

Who is part of your community, your support system, when it comes to adoption and parenting?
What are the benefits of surrounding yourself with those who can advise, encourage, and support you?

7

CONFIDENCE

"And this is the confidence that we have toward him, that if we ask anything according to his will he hears us."
1 John 5:14

I have never been a super popular person. I am not one who has tons of friends, but I have lots of acquaintances. To be honest, I am the worst person with names and even if I did have lots of friends, I would NEVER remember all of their names. I am blessed to say I have a hand full of really great girlfriends. The girls who were my bridesmaids in my wedding have been my friends since junior high and college. Though now I live far away from most of the friends I have had for more than ten years, we can call one another, no matter how long it has been and know we have not skipped a beat. I know and have every confidence that they are there for me. These girls have my back in every way. They knew me and loved me in my most awkward stages of Sally Jesse glasses and double slouched socks. They have loved me fat and loved me, well, not as fat. They are true, true, friends.

When my sweet hubby deployed with his fellow Green Berets and was in danger nearly every minute, I knew my girls were praying. When we struggled to begin our family I knew that even though they did not understand my journey that they would hop right along on it with me. When the adoption journey became a bumpy one and there were more questions than answers, I knew my girls were there for me and knowing they were brought me peace. Not just because I knew they would pray for me, and commiserate in a way that only best, longtime friends can but because I knew God had a role in it and I could feel Him there. I felt that God was truly in the midst of us. (See Matthew 18:20.)

I have to say, I truly felt strength in numbers, even small ones. I felt God was there and He heard not only my prayers but, the prayers of my friends on my behalf. I was confident He was there. I truly believed and held tight to the promise, "That if two of you shall agree on earth as touching anything that they shall ask, it shall be done for them of my Father which is in heaven." Matthew 18:19

Even now as a mommy to three, I call on my girlfriends. We call on each other. Someone's child needs help making better choices, another is hoping to get a part in a play, one has a concussion from Saturdays' game. There is always something and someone that needs us to pray for them. We still pray for each other but now the circle has widened and our children have come in.

There are so few things in life we can truly count on. So few people you know with every fiber of your being will be there for you, in your least glamorous non-exciting times, in your buried in a box of ice cream times, in the times that send you to your knees. But we all have "people". They do not have to be related to be your people, your family. I have several prayer warriors in my group of girlfriends and other friends have varying degrees of faith, but I had confidence that if I asked, they would pray WITH me.

Thank God for these amazing people He has brought into my lives; these people that have seen me at my best and worst and still love me. Find YOUR people. Pray with them. Let them pray for you. Have confidence in Him and know he is listening.

With ♥, safety pin friendship bracelets & rolled jeans-

Madeleine

Who has God sent you to pray with, that will also pray for you?
Do you have confidence that God is listening?
What is on your prayer list today?

8

CONTENTMENT

"You keep him in perfect peace whose mind is stayed on you,
because he trusts in you."
Isaiah 26:3

To be content. Seems like a lofty dream when you are in the midst of decisions, paperwork, e-mails and phone calls. Seems like a goal to be reached years down the road, when maybe, just maybe, that spare bedroom, the one where you keep the door closed, will contain toys and sunlight and the laughter of a child. Or maybe you think contentment will come when your child finally gets an accurate diagnosis or a better therapist.

When we were waiting for our first child, our profile was shown to more than fifteen expectant mothers who were considering making an adoption plan. I obsessively checked my voicemail and e-mail, hoping to hear from our social worker, and I begged God to end our wait soon and let us be chosen. I would torture myself by looking at the online profiles of other waiting hopeful adoptive parents, comparing myself to them. I was fully engulfed in adoption. The problem was that the jealousy, confusion, and desperation pulled me away from God and into a hurricane of self-service. I was trying to fill my aching heart with all the wrong things, thus denying myself true contentment.

God doesn't want us to put stipulations or a due date on contentment. Contentment is today's gift. It's here now. It's yours to claim.

But how, you ask, can contentment be claimed when you feel more like you are drowning rather than gracefully swimming in sparkly blue waters during a photo-worthy sunset? Isaiah 26:3 gives this advice: when a person's mind is on God, and stays on God, the gift of contentment (perfect peace) is bestowed. In exchange for trusting God, in His infinite wisdom and power and ability, we are given something that no piece of paper or phone call can give us.

We tend to complicate things, using human reasoning to try to figure out the puzzle adoption presents us. We wonder who, when, why, where? We have a lot of "what if" thoughts. We readily allow the fear of the unknown to consume us and steal the beauties of today. The perfect answer to every question, the response to every unknown, is to focus and refocus on Him. He will provide peace. His love never fails.

In contentment,
Rachel

What is hindering you today from embracing God's gift of contentment?
What does having true contentment mean for your today and tomorrows?

9

COURAGE

"Be strong and courageous. Do not fear or be in dread of them,
for it is the Lord your God who goes with you.
He will not leave you or forsake you."
Deuteronomy 31:6

Dorothy just wanted to go home. The Scarecrow desired a brain. The Tin Man wanted a heart. And the Lion, he wanted courage. With each frightening situation—facing an army of monkeys, confronting the Wicked Witch of the West, meeting the Great and Powerful Oz—the four-some came face-to-face with not only external situations and people, but they also had to face something that is often much scarier: themselves.

Much like Dorothy, the Scarecrow, the Tin Man, and the Lion, when you choose to adopt, you are going to face some big challenges. These challenges are not just big; they are also unpredictable and undesired. They creep up at the most inopportune times, forcing you to show your true colors. These situations beckon you. *What have you got on the inside? Do you have what it takes to push forward, or will you cower in fear and surrender?*

I'm friends with dozens of adoptive families, and I can tell you that not a single one has an adoption and parenting situation where it "went off without a hitch." There were my friends who traveled to Europe to adopt their son, but when arriving, learned he had already been adopted by another couple. They instead traveled to another nearby orphanage and adopted a daughter. There were the friends who were matched with an expectant mother for most of her pregnancy, yet when the baby was born, the mother quit communicating with the adoption agency and the prospective adoptive parents. There were our friends who were planning to adopt an infant girl with Down syndrome, but a month away from the baby being born, she died in utero. In each case, the prospective adoptive parents were left to face some tough stuff: loss, changes in plans, disappointment, confusion, grief, uncertainty. Many things that happen on a person's adoption journey are faith-shaking.

Deuteronomy 31:6 teaches us that God is for us. This doesn't mean things will always go our way. Instead, it means that whatever circumstances arise, we can be strong and courageous because He is with us. He will never give up on us and walk away. He won't stand with His back to us like a tantruming toddler. He won't throw insults at us like a rebellious teenager. His arms are always open, His ears always listening, His eyes always watching, His heart is ever widening.

In courage,
Rachel

At what point in your adoption or parenting journey did things "take a turn for the worst"?
What can you do the next time an unexpected adoption or parenting situation arises?

10

DISAPPOINTMENT

"And we know that for those who love God all things work together
for good, for those who are called according to his purpose."
Romans 8:28

Sometimes it is so hard to see that things will work out when you
are disappointed. I remember playing with a neighbor boy,
one of my best buddies in the second grade. All day we made
plans for a campout we were going to have in the backyard. We made
plans to use his tent, to forage for food in the backyard, and to come
up with enough money from our piggy banks to get marshmallows
for roasting. It was late afternoon when I finally presented this amazing plan to my mother, to which she answered, "No." I was shocked!
I had no idea why this plan we had put so much thought into was
seemingly so easily dismissed. How could the answer be, no? I did
not understand. I cried for several hours and obviously still remember that disappointment. At the time, I thought for sure my mother
had ruined my life.

So often with infertility, with the loss of children, with the journey to
adoption and with issues in parenting, we are taken by surprise when
our Father's answer is no. We are shocked and wonder, "Why? Why

is the answer, no?" Your plan makes so much sense. You have your life mapped out. You have made plans and have done what you are supposed to. Why couldn't your body carry a child or get pregnant? Why did the match not work in your adoption journey? Why is your travel postponed? Why did such small people have to go through so many adult problems in their first home? Such hard questions at the time. There seems to be no reasonable answer. And most of the time, if we ever find out "why", it is much later when HIS plan reveals itself.

Just weeks into our third adoption journey, we were presented with an opportunity to be considered for a child. I wanted it to feel right because I had wondered if with two children we would ever be chosen again. In the wee hours of the morning that we were to be presented, I was on the elliptical. A strong feeling came over me that that was not to be my child, that the answer was, "No." Even though calling our social worker and asking not to be presented felt like the right thing to do, I was so disappointed. What if another opportunity never presented itself?

Several weeks later, we were holding our son. God had another plan for us. God has a plan for you. In each "No," know that you are moving closer to your "Yes!". Like all parents, God does what is right for us and He truly sees the bigger picture. I know that a "no" is hard, but trust Him. Trust His plan. Your disappointment will only be temporary, but He is your Forever.

With ♥ & prayers for your "yes" moment-
Madeleine

Has God told you "NO" and it turned out for the better?
Do you turn towards God in your disappointments?
What questions are you asking God today? Has he answered you?

11

DISCERNMENT

"See to it that no one takes you captive by philosophy and empty deceit, according to human tradition, according to the elemental spirits of the world, and not according to Christ."
Colossians 2:8

My family's "adoption" status is apparent. My husband and I are White, and our children are Black. Whenever we go somewhere, whether we are dining in a restaurant, walking through an airport, or standing in line at a checkout lane in a store, we are often met with looks, questions, and comments regarding race and adoption. We have been asked if our kids are "real" siblings, why we chose to adopt (why we couldn't have "our own" children), how much adoption costs, how in the world do we take care of the girls' hair, how old their birth parents are, what country they are from, and much more. Most comments, questions, and looks are affirming or stem from curiosity, but some are intrusive, inappropriate, and just downright rude.

There will be many voices trying to "chime in" on your family choices. Some will not approve of you choosing to adopt. Some won't approve of you adopting a sibling group, a child with special needs, or a child who doesn't racially match you. Some will question your motives and decisions. You might be deemed a "hero" or "savior" because it's believed you "rescued" your children. Some might question why you adopted internationally when there are "so many children here who need a home." The many voices are polarizing and can shake your confidence as a parent or parent-to-be.

There are many misconceptions, stereotypes, and mysteries surrounding adoption. And there are also many opinions on why adoption is good or bad, necessary or unneeded, rewarding or dehumanizing. The many voices can confuse, frustrate, and annoy adoptive families, and furthermore, can seek to shame, isolate, and dishearten adoptees and birth families.

It's crucial that adoptive parents reject captivity "by philosophy and empty deceit" which is, according to Colossians, "human tradition," and instead focus on spiritual truths. To listen and take to heart every opinion and judgment that is thrown your way will only distract you from listening to God's promptings and the needs of your children.

With focus,
Rachel

Which voices have you listened to in the past, and how did those voices make you feel?
How can you realistically focus on God and not on the opinions of those who seek to distract you or tear down your family?

12

DOUBT

"Truly, I say to you, whoever says to this mountain, 'Be taken up
and thrown into the sea,' and does not doubt in his heart, but
believes that what he says will come to pass, it will be done for him.
Therefore I tell you, whatever you ask in prayer, believe that you
have received it, and it will be yours."
Mark 11: 23-24

There are certain points in time along the adoption journey
when your heart dips and your hopes wane. They are little
lows and sometimes huge gullies and with each you feel
you have lost a little bit of yourself. As if with each disappointment
the missing pieces grow. What if you made a little pile of rocks or
pebbles and each time something did not go as you had hoped, as
you had prayed, as you had secretly wished above all and tucked
so closely to your heart and it was not to be—what if then you add-
ed another rock, another pebble to that pile? When you looked at
that pile, what would you see? What would you feel? Would you feel
hopeless? Would you let all that doubt that you have been staving
off, creep in? Would you think of time and dreams lost? Of children
not to be? Would you let yourself think that you will never be the
parent you wanted to be? Would you drop to your knees, as I did so

many times along my own journey? I spent more time than I would like to admit in "ugly cry face, give me the chocolate and yes, maybe the wine, too", mode than I would like to admit to. I have been where you are. Hopeful. Sad. Faithful. Disappointed. Confused. Sometimes, angry. And then hopeful again.

And then there is that pile. What to do about the pile? In it may be opportunities when you were not chosen. Matches that were not to be. Children who left your home and did not return. Failed placements. Waits longer than you expected. Struggles with parenthood. Doubts about yourself that you have never had before. All those pieces of you. All those doubts and disappointments sitting in that pile. But what if that pile was part of the journey? An important part. What if that little pile was actually your mountain and you were at the peak? What if you were not really losing parts of you, but gaining parts you never knew you had? What if through all the doubts and disappointments you had built something?

A stronger relationship. A stronger faith. A stronger realization that you want to be a parent. A stronger feeling that you are who you need to be and where you need to be. A stronger you! It took a lot of time, a lot of prayer and a time of leaning on my husband's faith for me to come to these important realizations. I was stronger and you will be too when you let go of the doubt. Your tears do not make you weak-- Everything needs water to grow. You are strong. You have built this mountain! Whether you climb it or move it is your choice. You are on a strong foundation with God. Let some of that doubt go and believe in yourself and in the strength of your faith. You can come out of this, whole and stronger than when you began. BELIEVE.

I believe in you!

With ♥ & a mountain of my own-
Madeleine

What doubts are creeping into your adoption or parenting journey? In what ways have you found that the strength of your faith has lessened the doubts and made you stronger?

How will the pebbles of your journey, ultimately, make you a better person? Better parent? Better Christian?

13

ENCOURAGEMENT

"Therefore encourage one another and build one another up,
just as you are doing."
1 Thessalonians 5:11

When we were beginning the adoption process, we went to a meeting where our agency brought in a couple that had just recently come home with their child. It was just what I needed. I needed to see that in the midst of all that paperwork and fingerprints and portfolio creation there would eventually be a child. I needed to hear success stories. I needed to know that all the prayers, work, hoping, preparing, crying, believing were going somewhere. I needed comfort and encouragement, and I needed it most from people who understood. People who had been there.

I needed that same encouragement when our first little angel arrived in this world. I lost my mom a year before my son was born and while I had always been a rock star babysitter, I suddenly felt like I was a failure at being a mommy. Why was he crying? He had been fed, burped, changed, smiled at, rocked, sung to. Why? It must be me, I thought. My husband had to go back to our home state while I finished waiting out the ICPC (approval from the birth state to return to our home state). I felt incredibly alone until Anita, one of my best friends from college, said she would like to come visit us before we left. I looked and felt like a zombie at that point, but was beyond excited to see her. Shortly after she arrived we sat on the screened porch chatting. My little guy had been down for about fifteen minutes when tiny baby screams made their way through the monitor. I suddenly burst into tears, too. I told Anita my fears of being inept and with my ugliest cry face I blathered, "Why can't I just help him sleep? I am terrible at this!"

"You are not bad at this," she said, "He is a baby and babies do what babies want to. You are doing exactly what you are supposed to. You are a wonderful mommy. Don't be so hard on yourself. Babies cry. It is not you. It will get better and it will get different. You will do great!" It was exactly what I needed to hear; especially from someone I always thought was such a great mommy. I learned a lot on the encouragement of Anita, and my friend Tricia who was already juggling several children too. And my Grandma who could lay a crying baby on their belly over her lap and the baby would magically stop crying; I loved hearing her say I was doing a good job.

Parents can sometimes be tough on each other. Judging how others are raising their children rather than lifting each other up. In fact, helping each other when times are tough and complimenting each other on what we are doing right is what God wants. God wants us to comfort one another. God wants us to encourage one another, and God wants to encourage you, too! God does not want you to lose heart or be discouraged when times are tough. Look at Jesus, His story, the story of a man who went as far as to die on the cross. He who endured such pain and yet is now seated at the right hand of God.

Be encouraged. Be an encourager. Be that big warm blanket that makes others feel good. Be that person that allows themselves to open their ears and heart when another is lending a story or wisdom that can help. Be open to being encouraged. Watch and expect that God will provide exactly what you need today.

With ♥ and a whole heaping pile of encouragement-
Madeleine

Do you encourage others who are around you?
What do you need encouragement about today?
Do you allow yourself to be encouraged by scripture?
Are you open to exactly what God is providing you today?

14

ENDURANCE

"Therefore, since we are surrounded by so great a cloud of
witnesses, let us also lay aside every weight, and sin which clings so
closely, and let us run with endurance the race that is set before us."
Hebrews 12:1

Being a mother to multiple young children is exhausting.
There are days when time drags on so slowly and the chaos is
so loud that all I can do is pray for the moment my husband
walks in the door and we can tag-team the parental duties. There have
been days when my blood sugars roller coaster, and I'm left groggy,
shaky, angry, and frustrated. Some days I feel like I'm being pulled
in one hundred directions all at once: the phone won't stop ringing,
e-mails pour in from editors, the kids have classes and lessons to at-
tend, and the van is making a concerning and threatening noise.

If there is one thing you need for certain along your adoption
and parenting journey, it's endurance. You can place a bet, which
is a guaranteed win, that your patience and your faith will be tested
many times.

It's quite tempting to throw in the proverbial towel when the going gets tough. Sometimes you want to crawl under your comforter
and hide from the responsibilities and demands of life, hibernating

like a bear and hoping when you wake up everything will be magically better. But you cannot, because the dishes are still dirty, the kids need to eat dinner, and you still have work deadlines that are fast-approaching. You might have a child who is struggling with a traumatic past, a pending adoption that keeps getting delayed, or a spouse who isn't sure if adoption is the right path for your family.

Hebrews tells us that we need to "lay aside every weight" and every "sin which clings so closely" and "run with endurance the race that is set before us." I know. Sounds impractical, right? Just throw aside sin and hindrances and sprint through a sunny field of roses toward greater tomorrows, our capes fluttering behind us in the spring breeze.

Let me tell you how this verse speaks to me. It tells me that I have a choice in the matter, because it says "let us." Let us make the decision to cast aside all of life's distractions, life's extras, the things that we weren't meant to carry. Set them aside so that we can focus on what matters most, what is truly demanded of us. We are able to do this with God's grace and strength.

Running,
Rachel

What "extras" do you need to lay aside so you can focus on what truly matters?
Society tells us to "grin and bear" challenges (aka: "fake it 'til you make it"), but God offers endurance. How do you define endurance?

15

FAITH

"It is like a grain of mustard seed, which, when sown on the ground,
is the smallest of all the seeds on earth, yet when it is sown it grows
up and becomes larger than all the garden plants and puts out large
branches, so that the birds of the air can make nests in its shade."
Mark 4:31-32

My mom was preparing to make a great leap of faith. It was just moments before she would descend my great aunt and uncle's beautiful spiral staircase to marry a second time. I was a newly graduated sixth grader, waiting, clad in my peach and white islet dress and a ring of dried flowers adorning my Mary Lou Retton haircut. My mom came to me, with a necklace in her hand. The pendant looked like a clear teardrop at first glance, but once I looked closer I could see something inside. My mom explained that it was a mustard seed. *Strange choice for a necklace*, I thought. When you are 11 you think most things your parents do are strange. She went on to explain the parable of the mustard seed. I looked at how tiny it was. So little. How could it grow to be so strong? It did not look like anything miraculous. Hard to believe it could do anything at all, really.

It was not until I was an adult that I realized how far a little faith could go. I had been raised with faith and known it was strong, but as an adult it continued to be tested. Boyfriends not working out. My mom's illness and death. My husband's deployments. My hope for a child. The stresses of an adoption journey. I had worried that when my mom died I would lose my faith. I did not. I think I leaned on it, just as I did through much of our journey to becoming parents. Shortly before we became parents for the first time, I crumbled. I spent many hours in what was to be the nursery, praying- hoping- wondering-worrying-crying. I was not putting my full faith in God. It was then that my husband, so new to his faith, allowed me to lean on him. He carried us with his faith for a time. That little mustard seed became strong. We remembered that God was there for us and what- ever happened God would get us through. It is the same faith that I now, as a mommy to three, lean on with all the parenting "what if's" I face daily. My faith is the greatest gift my mom ever gave me and I am passing that gift on to my children. I could not get through a single day without that gift of faith.

When you feel low, when you are discouraged, when you wonder if you can move forward, draw on your faith: that belief in that which you cannot see. That mustard seed has served me well and it is bound to serve you well.

♥, hugs, and a mustard seed-
Madeleine

How has your faith been tested?
What things have grown your faith over time?
Is your faith as strong as it could be?

16

FORGIVENESS

"Be kind to one another, tenderhearted, forgiving one another, as
God in Christ forgave you."
Ephesians 4:23

My oldest two children, both girls who are two years apart in
age, have frequent sisterly spats. They can be best friends
one minute, playing happily with toys, and the next minute they are bickering over the slightest infraction. Each time this
happens, I ask them what occurred, and when I discover who chose
to harm the other, an apology is an order. The children know our
routine well enough. They must look one another in the eye, and the
offender says, "I'm sorry" and the other child says, "I forgive you." It
is usually after this, when we are able to discuss the situation and offer forgiveness and acceptance, that the kids are able to go back to
playing like nothing ever happened.

But forgiveness seems to rarely work out this well for adults. We
forgive but hold on to resentment. We forgive fifty-percent. We forgive while clinging to self-righteousness. We forgive with reservation.
We forgive but continue to talk badly about the person who hurt us.

True, full-fledged forgiveness is essential when you are an adoptive parent. There will be times someone has harmed your child,

intentionally or not, and you will have the choice: forgive and move forward with the right attitude and heart-set, or dwell on the wrongdoing and allow your anger to become your child's legacy. Sometimes you will have to forgive when forgiveness wasn't asked for. Sometimes you will have to forgive because it's that or let the darkness of the situation take root in your heart for the long-haul. Sometimes you will have to forgive because you are modeling for your children what forgiveness is and why it is important.

Whether you are forgiving a family member who said something negative about your child's adoption story, or you are forgiving your child's birth mother for choosing to drink throughout her pregnancy, or you are forgiving a stranger for the inappropriate adoption terminology he used, it boils down to you: *you* are forgiving, just as "God in Christ forgave you." With forgiveness comes a heart-set that is life-changing: one of kindness and tenderness. What a tremendous gift to give your child!

With a tender heart,
Rachel

Who are you struggling to forgive?
How can asking God to assist you in forgiving this person help you move forward with the right heart-set?

17

GRACE

"But if it is by grace, it is no longer on the basis of works; otherwise
grace would no longer be grace."
Romans 11:6

Sometimes the road to parenthood is a bumpy and we may feel
we are not being the person we want to be; that we are not worthy of a child. Our thoughts may turn negative. We are not embracing the world with our usual kindness. We wonder what we can
do, what we can change in ourselves to make things better. The same
can be said once we become parents. No matter how much we hope
and prayed for these little people, parenting is hard. We are human
beings. We get tired. We lose patience. We feel inept. Our children
can make us crazy. Exasperated. Exhausted.

School mornings at my house are enough to make the sanest,
most patient human being want to go back to bed and pull the covers
over their head. One child is up when it is still dark outside and wants
a four course breakfast. The other two won't get up until there are no
more than 10 minutes before they have to get out the door. It is a mad
frenzy of food, searching for the backpack I told them to hang on the
hook the night before, morning hair taming and me repeating the
same instructions as I do every other school day for the 8-billionth

time. "Get in the car!" I bellow into the air at least 4 times before everyone is piled in. By the time I am in the car, I am ready for them to go to school. It's 8 a.m. and I am sometimes irritated but always exhausted and tired of my own voice. But no matter how frustrated I am, when those little darlings get out of the car, I always say, "Do your best today! I love you!" Because not matter what day we are having, that is the constant. Nothing takes from my love for them. Nothing.

No matter who you are today or how disappointed you are in yourself or your choices, God loves you and has given you HIS grace. He loves you no matter what you do or have done. He loves you and there is nothing you can physically do to make Him love you more. Be happy in knowing it, just as your children will find comfort in knowing the same is true for your love of them. Constant, steadfast and sure. Unwavering. Your child's love will be the same. Children can be hardest on those that they know will always be there for them, those that love them- no matter what.

When you finally realize there's nothing you can do to make God love you more, it is one of the most freeing feelings in the world. Every day, remind yourself of the grace of God, and allow yourself to breathe. There is no greater gift than the grace we are given by our Lord. I regularly tell my children that I make mistakes. That I am human. Those sweet little people can be very hard on themselves sometimes when they have done something wrong. They should know that parents mess up too. They should know that God loves us anyway. Being good doesn't get you more love, just as making mistakes or poor choices does not get you less. Your child did not have to earn your love. God feels the same way about you. He loves you because you exist. He loves you because you are HIS. He loves you because you are you and nothing good or bad can change that. Nothing! So remember to extend yourself some grace. Extend some grace to your spouse, your children, the person that cut you off in traffic. It IS what God does for us, every moment of every day.

One of the purest Christian definitions of GRACE is that it is the "bestowal of blessings." Try and remember today, no matter what happens, how blessed you really are.

With ♥ & so many blessings for your week-
Madeleine

Are you allowing yourself to embrace the grace God has given you? If not, what can you do to remind yourself?
Do you give those around you the same grace that you are given?

18

GRACIOUSNESS

"Gracious words are like a honeycomb, sweetness to the soul and
health to the body."
Proverbs 16:24

I never heard my mom speak poorly about anyone. I never heard
her share gossip. The latest news of the circles she was in? Yes.
You know, whose daughter was pregnant, and whose was getting
married, which friends were going on vacation- but never gossip. She
never said anything she would have to whisper, unless someone was
sick or had died. She always had a kind word for others and her real
estate customers always returned when they bought or sold again because of the person she was.

When my sweet mama left this world, so many people shared stories with my sister and I about how she had touched their lives or
someone else's. The new stylish coat she had just gotten when she was
a school girl and gave to another child who was in need. The gifts she
always purchased for older children on the angel tree at Christmas
because they were so often forgotten. The uplifting words she always
had for a friend. The absence of judgment.

Another wonderfully gracious woman, my mom's friend Cathy, share
the eulogy at my mom's funeral. She spoke of unpacking boxes when my

parents moved into their new home when I was in my twenties. The same boxes filled with family crystal also had Mason jars carefully wrapped in them. And that is who my sweet mama was: unassuming, not putting one thing above another. She had wrapped both the crystal and the jars carefully as they were both fragile. Mingling both together because that is who she was. If only the same could be said for all of us. What if all of us had a kind word to share? What if we all made the choice to reach out to others, without judgment and find something nice to say? What if we saw that everyone can be fragile and everyone has worth? Don't we like to be around other people who take interest in us, ask how we are doing or feeling and really listen to how we respond?

God treats us with the same care whether we see ourselves as a Mason jar or crystal glass. God expects us to be kind. Whether you are meeting with a group of people who are also praying to be a parent through adoption: you are in a waiting parents or parents Facebook group, or you are chatting with a friend or family member, you will be a happier person, and it will be "healing to the bones" of not just you, but the person you are speaking to, if you choose gracious words. Be the unassuming Mason jar. Speak without judgment and really engage in what the other person is saying, rather than planning what you will say next.

There are different ways to adopt. There are different ways to parent and each child comes with their own personal set of challenges. Let's not judge, but instead, make the effort to be that jar of honey. We are on this adoption and parenting journey together and quite unmerited, have all been saved by God's gracious intervention on our behalf. It is only fitting we try to be gracious, as well.

With ♥ and honey-
Madeleine

Can you speak to and about others without a whisper?
Are your words a honeycomb? Do you choose to be around others who are?
Who can you lift up this week with your kind words and understanding?

19

GRATITUDE

" rooted and built up in him and established in the faith, just as you
were taught, abounding in thanksgiving."
Colossians 2:7

I recently read a post on social media that said, "What if you woke
up tomorrow and only had what you had been thankful for the
day before." Good gravy! That could be a problem! I think some
weeks that would leave me with very little, were this statement true.
Sometimes it is easier to let out all of the complaints we have, or to
spend our time in prayer with the requests and burdens that are on
our hearts, forgetting how important it is to be thankful. To share
with God the gratitude of what we do have, rather than to only focus
on what we feel we do not.

When we were waiting to adopt the first time, I spent a lot of
my time worrying, wondering, hoping and praying. Very few of those
were prayers were full of gratitude and thanksgiving for the many
blessings I already had. My journey would have had a little more sun-
shine if I had taken the time each day to be thankful even if I was
struggling? Don't we feel better when we say positive things out loud

or let our heart scream them out for us! Why don't we do that more? When we are hearing "no" that does not take from all the times we have heard "yes."

Once I became a parent I was a giant bundle of gratitude. I could have danced everywhere I went, kissed random older gentlemen on their bald heads and sung show tunes and hymns from the top of my lungs. But as the realities of motherhood and sleepless nights and zombie days set in, I lost focus. Sometimes it is so hard to see beyond our latest worry, problem, or fixation. Sometimes we become so busy with the children, career concerns, housework, and ball games that we do not make time to be thankful. How much better would our lives and our outlooks be if we spent more time in thanksgiving to God? To truly be thankful for all we have been given?

I quickly became unsettled recently as my darling children were wild and had to be told everything five times before school. (Moms of twelve-year-old boys, how many times did you say, "Did you brush your teeth? GO brush your teeth!" this morning before school? And where are all the shoes, really?!?) Then, the dishwasher repairman finally came with the new part, only to break another part in the process of installing it and suddenly I heard I could not use it at all for at least a week. Ugh, dishes for five. Once he left and I finished sweeping up the remnants of breakfast grumbling to myself that it looked like the kids had a food fight. Then it dawned on me. I thought, *what first world problems I have! How lucky am I to have these issues? To have food on the table and clean water to wash dishes with and to have the children that my heart longed for, for what seemed like a lifetime.*

I am still cleaning up my children's breakfast crumbs each day and may be asking my son if he has brushed his teeth until he is eighteen, but I am doing it with the gentle hum of gratitude. Can you look at your blessings, big and small and find the inspiration for a lil' show tune or a thankful heart song?

I am grateful for YOU today!

With ♥ & gratitude for my now working dishwasher {and for toothpaste}-
Madeleine

What can you be thankful for?
Do you show gratitude and thanksgiving, even when things are not going your way?
What is keeping you from showing your gratitude and singing out your thankful heartsong, everyday?

20

HEARTACHE

"The LORD is near to the brokenhearted and
saves the crushed in spirit."
Psalm 34:18

If there is one common thread that runs through every adoption, it's heartache. Many times adoptive parents choose to adopt because of infertility, infant loss, or miscarriage. Biological parents place children for a variety of reasons, but it may include a lack of stability or a support system, financial struggles, age, and ability. Children who are placed for adoption have no say-so in the matter and down the road may face questions of "why" and perhaps may search for his or her biological family.

All of these situations can cause tremendous heartache, both temporary and continual. And heartbreak can be debilitating and life-altering.

What is a person to do when is experiencing a broken heart? Or what if you are the parent of a child who is struggling with an abusive or neglectful past, loss or confusion stemming from the adoption, or you are perhaps part of an open adoption where you are aware of the birth parent's heartache?

Heartache can be quite isolating. One reason I believe this is true is because most people wear a mask each day, concealing what's going on in their hearts. Sometimes this is necessary. After all, there are still bills to pay, work to be accomplished, relationships to maintain. Life happens whether or not we are actively participating. But when we pass by one another in stores, in the hallways at work, while picking up our kids from school, we don't often think about the weight each of us is carrying around.

Psalm 34:18 offers a simple and mighty statement: that God is right by us when our hearts break and fall to pieces. He saves those who have a crushed spirit.

It may not feel like it right now, in the midst of your heart breaking, but God is near. He hasn't forgotten you. He knows the depth and weight of your pain. He's not finished with you. And He needs you, in His strength, to hang on to what you know to be true: Him. In an ever-changing world, there is only one Constant, one King, one Deliverer, one Savior. And that One chooses to be near *you*.

With a healing heart,
Rachel

What has broken or is breaking your heart when it comes to adoption or parenting?
Where is the place you can go, or the thing you can do, in which you always feel close to God, where you inevitably feel His mighty presence and peace?

21

HERITAGE

"Behold, children are a heritage from the Lord,
the fruit of the womb a reward."
Psalms 127:3

When each of my children were placed in my arms, I thought there could not have been a more darling, perfect, blanket full of wrinkles, smells and smiles in the world. Perfect. No doubt, even as newborns, my kids were the smartest, best most wonderfulest (were that a word) human beings in all the land. I could have looked at those sweet little faces and hands and toes forever. Children truly are a heritage from the Lord. Plainly said, they are a gift. Some in the adoption community will tell you it is not okay to call a child a gift either to yourself or from a birth parent, but truth be told children, all children, are a gift from God to the world.

I was adopted. Knowing I was adopted was much like having a belly button: it was just always there. Growing up, I often shared my adoption story with others in the neighborhood or at school. My story was just how I came to be with my family. It was my truth, just as some people may be a twin or might have been born prematurely. My own sweet mommy was never shy about expressing her thankfulness for my adoption or our family story. She said she had a tummy ache for the whole twenty-four hours before I arrived to her following the social workers call- that is how excited she was for me to arrive! Nor did she shy from telling me what I blessing I was. Not because I was adopted, but because I was me and she was so happy to love me. I was truly celebrated every day in a million different ways. Every child should be.

If you are feeling low; feeling so incredibly unworthy of God's reward and of His amazing grace and all He provides, remember that you too are a heritage from the Lord. We are all His children, and He will provide us with what we need. If you are waiting to adopt I know you already have an inkling of the love you will burst wide open when your child arrives. If you are already parenting, I know you know how you suddenly seem to exude love from every nook and cranny for that child that might as well have hung the moon (no matter what smells they make!).

If you are waiting for God's reward, please do not think in any way that the reward is only for those who are perfect in some part of their life. I am not perfect, yet by God's grace have known so many joys in my life, not the least of which my three children. Children just like anything else God provides come without our truly being worthy. Remember, you started out as a child; we are ALL a heritage of the Lord. God was just as excited to see your face and to see you arrive to this world. He wants to provide for you just as you will or do provide for your child.

Going through the adoption process, one truly comes to appreciate the gift that children are. EVERY child is a gift. Whether they were adopted, a preemie, one of three triplets or the tenth child of twelve in the family, they are all gifts. My babies are much bigger now; their little faces have changed (so have their smells) and all but one have lost the dimples on those little hands but they will always be "my babies". Whether they throw a fit before school, refuse to eat their veggies or even if your child struggles with bigger issues they are ours and they came from Him. He feels the same way about YOU, too! I have a sign that says, Children are a heritage of the Lord, in my own home with my sweet babies' little pre-school pictures hanging under it. Oh how I love those sweet lil' cheeks. They are a blessing; even on their worst days- don't we all want to be that to God? To each other?

I am saying a prayer of thanksgiving right now for my children, as well as yours and those you are hoping for. God is so good in sharing these amazing little humans with us. No matter how imperfect you feel as a parent or a Christian, remember; God celebrates you, His child, and all of his children. No one better knows your heart or what you need, more than God and no parent has ever loved His children more than He has loved us. We are the heritage of the Lord and will always share that heritage with our children. Feeling humbled yet? I sure am!

With ♥ exuding from my nooks and crannies-
Madeleine

Do you allow yourself to be human embracing the fact that you too are a gift from God?

If you are waiting to adopt do you struggle with the feeling of being unworthy? How so?

How can you ready yourself to receive the gift of a child? Or, if you are already a parent, are you fully rejoicing in the heritage God has blessed you with?

22

HOPE

"And we know that for those who love God all things work together
for good, for those who are called according to his purpose."
Romans 8:28

Before we ever had children, I surprised my hubby with a private deep sea fishing trip for his birthday. We left our hotel room the day we were to set sail, excited and looking forward to the next hours out on the ocean. I grew up going to the beach and sometimes sailing the inlet with my Uncle Bob and Aunt Marsha on their little boat. Not once had I ever felt sick or woozie when I was out to sea. I have a father who really sails tall boats that are out to sea for weeks. Of course I had sea legs, right? Needless to say I was shocked when the deep sea fishing boat I hired made it out just a few miles from dock and I felt as though I may lose my breakfast all over the ship deck. I excused myself and laid down on the seats inside the cabin. I could not wait until the boat stopped somewhere. I wanted it to anchor more than anything so I could get my bearings. So I could be strong and move along with my day. I was resting my vacation on this anchor that I could not even see and did not have any control over- but I knew I needed it.

We need an anchor of hope along our adoption journey too. Hebrews 6:19 says, "We have this as a sure and steadfast anchor of the soul, a hope that enters into the inner place behind the curtain." The soul is the ship being cast about on the sea. Our hope is the anchor which rests on our faith and God's promises are the cable that connects the two. Our anchor would do us no good in this choppy world, without the rope that ties us to it. It is a difficult concept for me to wrap my head around. To the world, hope is a kind of cross your fingers and toes, wear your lucky socks and let the wind blow just right and maybe, just maybe it could happen for you. The Bible shares hope as more of a promise that comes with faith and with God. It is something that will be fulfilled. What if we could all look at things that way? What if our faith in the way the Bible portrays hope, released us from all of the fixating and for some of us, chocolate eating, which comes with waiting to see if our hope comes to fruition and becomes our reality.

I am a planner to the nth degree. I have little lists and sticky notes, schedules and color coded calendars. I like to know ahead of time what I am going to be doing and at what time and will probably think ahead about what I am going to wear for said event. It is who I am. When I need something done, I am most likely to do it myself. So to rely on anyone or anything or to not have a sure thing through all my own hard work is hard for me. To HOPE seems risky. My hope in things comes with many question marks. It is hard to "hope" and not just "do". That made the adoption process very difficult for me. I could take charge of my giant binder and checklists for our home-study. I could put together our adoption profile, just so and could accept or walk away from a match but beyond that I had not control. All I could do was hope and pray and lean on my faith.

If we look at hope as the promise it is made to be in the Bible how different would our journey be? Could we stop worrying and fretting? Could we just prepare for the future without all the negatives in our head? Could we open our hearts wider to receive the promise? Could we just take God at His word? Could hope be our anchor? When I put it that way, it makes it kind of hard not to, doesn't it?

Hope does not mean you do not do anything on your end. Of course you cannot just HOPE to adopt without completing your home study. You cannot just HOPE your child will be polite without teaching them. You cannot just HOPE to be a good parent without working at it. You cannot hope the dirty socks will hop into the hamper. God does expect us to do our part and there is no doubt he will do His. God keeps his promises and HOPE is one of them.

With ♥ and my anchor secured to Him-
Madeleine

In what ways do you let your faith hold up your hope?
How are you doing your part for what it is you are hoping for?
How can you better take God at His word?

23

INVITATION

"he predestined us for adoption as sons through Jesus Christ,
according to the purpose of his will,"
Ephesians 1:5

I loved my children before I ever knew them. I loved them before I ever saw them. I knew that when they came to me I would give them all that I had, without question. I would be theirs. My heart and mind were prepared to receive these precious children, no invitation needed, kind of like just walking in the front door at your Mee-Maw's house. No formal invitation needed. Just a joyful face and big ol' bear hug when you got in.

There is a point in the finalization of adoptions when the judge says something to the parents who are adopting the child to ensure they understand that once finalization is complete, the child will be theirs in every way. That he or she will be your son or daughter and carry your name. Your child will be entitled to receive anything willed by you and of course are your responsibility to feed and clothe and care for. I was ready. I did not need to be told or reminded. I did not need a formal invitation; my heart had already embraced these sweet lil' people in every way. I did not need to be questioned about my commitment to each of my sweet babies. There was nothing more in the world that I wanted to do than to be their mommy. I wanted each to be my sons and daughter, forever and I was ready to take the good with the bad, just as we do when we take our marriage vows. Ready to share a name, a home, a life. My children did not have to jump through hoops or prove themselves. I never said "Oh no! Only perfect children can be loved and raised in my house!"

What is amazing is that God did the same for us. When he created us he could have made us anything. He could have chosen for us to be his slaves if he had wanted to, but instead he chose for us to be His children. He chose to love and care for us in a way that only a Father could. We could have been anything to Him, yet he chose for us to be His sons and daughters. He never said we had to be perfect (and thank goodness for that because who could measure up?) In all of our glorious imperfection, God adopted all of us! (Titus 3:7)

You have been invited, though you never needed an invitation. Whether you are hungry, lost, hurting, desperate, waiting. joyful. He is there. He is ready to wrap you in his embrace, because just as it happens in adoption, loving and accepting before we even know our children, God loves and accepts you. HE is there for you. You may invite a birth family into your fold as a part of open adoption or take in children who have experienced trauma in their little lives. Your heart can open wider than you think. Your love can be unconditional and your arms outstretched, like God's. No formal invitation needed.

With ♥ & Mee-Maw hugs,
Madeleine

Do you speak to God as your Father, the Father who chose you, when you need guidance?
Do you need an invitation to love fully, including yourself, every day?
Do you invite others in when you are down?

24

ISOLATION

"Whoever isolates himself seeks his own desire; he breaks out against all sound judgment."
Proverbs 18:1

Adoption and isolation often go hand-in-hand. For one, no two adoption journeys are alike. Even if you are friends with other adoptive families, their stories won't be your story. Second, adoption often earns families one of two labels: heroes or anomalies. Either can be ostracizing, encouraging isolation. Finally, many children come from traumatic situations, so as families cope with their child's behaviors and work to meet the child's needs, isolation can be a natural result.

Isolation happens organically for many, but it's not a place to relish in. Proverbs warns us that isolation is a selfish ambition. Isolation creates an environment of foolishness, and of course, choosing foolishness can lead to dire consequences, both personally and for those around you, including the child you adopt.

When we initially chose to adopt, we knew three local adoptive families. Their insight was valuable to us, but more so, simply interacting with these families and feeling a sense of inclusion and commonality was encouraging. After we were placed with our first child, I started an adoptive mom support group that grew from just ten women to now well over two-hundred and fifty. To this day, any concern, question, or idea I have can be presented to the group for feedback.

Who can a prospective or current adoptive parent lean on when challenges arise? What is the appropriate response when one is feeling jealous of friends who are having baby after baby? What should a couple do when they are facing their third failed adoption? What about when the beloved foster child goes back to her biological family after being with you for two years?

Isolation is not the answer. It's a slippery slope. The opposite of isolation is community. Be ready, friend. Have your village on standby. Your village of other adoptive or foster families. Your village of friends who won't judge your raw emotions. Your family members who are eagerly waiting, alongside you, for the day you get the long-awaited phone call from your social worker.

In community,
Rachel

What challenge are you facing right now in your adoption on parenting journey that is nudging you toward choosing isolation over community?
What practical steps can you take to avoid isolating yourself when difficulties arise?

25

JEALOUSY

"A tranquil heart gives life to the flesh,
but envy makes the bones rot."
Proverbs 14:30

Envy is inevitable part of adoption. There will be a time or two (or one hundred) when you will feel jealous of someone else. It might be your cousin who announces she's pregnant with her third child, your co-worker who found out she's having twins, the magazine-cover-worthy couple at the mall cooing at their six-month-old baby in the stroller, or a stranger-couple on your adoption agency's website who was matched with an expectant mother before you. You may "grin and bear it" when you hear someone else's happy news, but inside you are furious or deeply saddened.

The problem with envy isn't the fact that you feel it. The problem is when you invite envy to make its home within you, occupying your thoughts and dictating not only your mood, but your overall state of heart and mind. Or, as Proverbs warns us, "makes the bones rot." Envy can cause our good sense to deteriorate, leaving us feeling and acting rotten.

When we were waiting to adopt our first child, we joined an agency branch that had just opened. We started waiting alongside another couple. I was giddy with excitement when our profile went live on the agency's website, but a few days later, I was overwhelmed with envy when I saw the other couple's profile had "matched" stamped across their photograph. What was wrong with us? What was so great about this other couple? I scoured their profile and found nothing remarkable about them, so why were they chosen and we weren't? The real icing on the cake was when this couple was not only placed once, but twice, while we continued to wait for our first child.

I found that my bitterness, stemming from jealousy, did nothing put poison my soul and distract me from enjoying my life. It was after several months of feeling envious that I realized I had control over my own actions. I stopped looking at online profiles of waiting couples. I chose to stop torturing myself and start focusing on readying my heart and home for our future child. I found what Proverbs refers to as tranquility. It certainly wasn't easy to choose tranquility over envy, and it was a choice I had to make many times over the course of waiting to adopt three children.

In tranquility,
Rachel

What triggers jealousy in you?
What are some healthy ways you can cope with jealousy when it arises so that you can instead choose tranquility?

26

JOY

"Count it all joy, my brothers, when you meet trials of various kinds,
for you know that the testing of your faith produces steadfastness."
James 1:2- 3

I loved going to Bible camp as a kid and I loved playing bells in the choir. I have never forgotten the song I learned in third grade: "God Loves a Cheerful Giver." One of the verses (which I would gladly sing for you, were you here as it is remembered from circa 1980) shares: "God loves a cheerful giver, give it all you've got! He loves to hear you laughing when you're in an awkward spot. When the odds are up against you- it's time to stop and sing! Praise God for to praise Him is a joyous thing!"

When the Bible speaks to being a cheerful giver, if references giving to the church, "Each one must give as he has decided in his heart, not reluctantly or under compulsion, for God loves a cheerful giver." 2 Corinthians 9:7 But being a cheerful giver can relate to more than tithing. God wants your heart in a happy way of your choosing. This scripture can actually relate to all of our spiritual walk with God, every day we have here on this Earth.

Turns out that being a cheerful giver is not always easy. The hardest part can be- the singing through an awkward spot or when the odds are up against you. How do you do that? That means finding the joy. There are times of trouble, disappointment and worry, times when we are having a hard time functioning, much less doing it with a smile. Add on the pressure of joy (which seems like happy on steroids), and that almost seems too much to ask! When I think JOY my initial thoughts are of newborn babies, 97th birthday celebrations, big job promotions, weddings when you know the couple is perfect for one another, losing two pounds even though you ate half a batch of cookies, but these things don't happen every day. What about the other days?

What do you do on the tough days? The days you are waiting for an answer? The days you have gotten the answer and it was not what you hoped for? The days when you feel like you should have stayed in bed? These are the days God wants you to find praise, to find joy, and to find thanksgiving. It might be in a sunset or giant moon outside your door. It might come from a stranger holding the door, a toddler waving little dimpled hands and smiling at you in the grocery store, or getting a real hand-written card in the mail. It is true we can usually find things to be thankful for even when things are tough, but we have to really hunt for the joy. Joy is not something you can fake and we cannot wait for a celebration or a baby to find it. It is there, in every day, in praising God, in being thankful for all we do have. In sharing a smile, encouragement, faith or something you can touch. It is amazing what singing a favorite song at the top of your lungs in the car can do for your disposition! So whether you are waiting for an answer, struggling with the daily ins and outs of parenting or figuring out what to do when the answer was, "no", don't forget the joy. And for goodness sakes, don't forget to share it.

With ♥ and praising God ("for to praise Him is a joyous thing!"),
Madeleine

In what moments do you find it hardest to find joy? How can you turn it around?
What will you find joy in today?
Do you take time each day to praise God? How?

27

LOSS

"Blessed are those who mourn, for they shall be comforted."
Matthew 5:4
"fear not, for I am with you; be not dismayed, for I am your God;
I will strengthen you, I will help you, I will uphold you with my
righteous right hand."
Isaiah 41:10

I remember being outside sledding with friends when I sipped on the ice in my friend's driveway. My feet went out from under me and I landed flat on my back on the concrete. Every bit of air in my body seemed to be gone and I could not find it. I could not only, not catch my breath; it seemed to just be gone. What was probably seconds, felt like an eternity, wondering if I would breathe again. This is really the only way I can think of to explain loss. Whether you have mourned a child through miscarriage, have mourned your fertility, or mourned the plans you had that were not meant to be, you know that feeling: wondering if you will ever breathe again. Unless you have ever had that dream, that wish, that prayer for a child and then lost that little life, could not create one or saw your chance at a family crumble before you, you just cannot imagine it. You cannot know those seasons of loss and grief; those moments on the floor in a heap.

I wish it were not true, but children are not exempt from grief or loss. Children in care have often lost their childhood to circumstances beyond their control. Some abused. Some exposed to things a child should never see or hear. Their innocence is often lost and these children are left to battle that trauma. These children have been bounced around and eventually lost their birth family. These sweet children have lost time with people they could call family, who would love them forever. Tiny tears from children, some of whom have never owned their own pillows. My heart is breaking, just typing about them.

And there are birthparents. I knew that even if I were offered the chance, I would not choose to be in the delivery room when any of my children were born. It did not seem like the kind or fair thing to do to be there. My heart was so filled with joy it was something that could not be contained. All the while, a birthparent's heart is breaking. Giving birth but going home with empty arms. Breathless. I could not bring my joy into the place where another person was pouring their heart out onto the floor. It is the expectant parent's moment, whether it is of pride, joy, accomplishment or utter devastation and loss.

As I laid on my back in my friends driveway, waiting for my breath to return, it felt as though I was all alone as I looked up to the empty sky. The truth is though, we are never alone. Not even in our grief. God does hear you. His answer may just come differently than you had hoped or expected. My mom always said that she never regretted not being able to carry a pregnancy easily, because if she had, she would not have me. No doubt God found a way to answer her prayers, just not as she expected.

As you grieve the loss of the plan you had for yourself or you work to help your child with the losses they have known, let God be the rock. Let Him be your fortress, your stronghold, your deliverer and salvation (Psalm 18:2). Let Him hold you up when you feel you cannot stand for one more minute. Pour out your troubles so you have room for the joy to come. You will breathe again. And when His plan has been revealed (Romans 8:18) and when you have found comfort, reach out and comfort those who have just lost their breath.

"Blessed be the God and Father of our Lord Jesus Christ, the Father of mercies and God of all comfort, who comforts us in all our affliction, so that we may be able to comfort those who are in any affliction, with the comfort with which we ourselves are comforted by God." Corinthians 1:3-4

♥, huge hugs, and a little oxygen-
Madeleine

What have you done to work through the loss and grief that either brought you to your adoption journey or has occurred along it?
In what ways has God revealed His plan?
What have you done to help others around you to catch their breath?

28

LOVE

"Beloved, let us love one another, for love is from God, and whoever loves has been born of God and knows God. Anyone who does not love does not know God, because God is love. In this the love of God was made manifest among us, that God sent his only Son into the world, so that we might live through him. In this is love, not that we have loved God but that he loved us and sent his Son to be the propitiation for our sins. Beloved, if God so loved us, we also ought to love one another. No one has ever seen God; if we love one another, God abides in us and his love is perfected in us. By this we know that we abide in him and he in us, because he has given us of his Spirit. And we have seen and testify that the Father has sent his Son to be the Savior of the world."
1 John 4:7-14

There is no doubt that love comes from God. In a million different ways He has shown it to us; saving us, forgiving us, calling us His children, allowing His own son to die for our sins! I also think God's love extends out into our lives through other people He has chosen to cross our path. As an adoptee and a mommy through adoption I have seen and felt God's love from so many places. There is the love of some birth parents, like mine, who I believe make a choice for their child that is predicated in love. There is the love of foster parents which I was also blessed to have been cared for by and loved by, though they knew I would not always be there. There is the love I knew from my parents, welcoming me with open arms and hearts, and giving me a forever home. There is the love of my little sister. A sister I share not a bit of DNA with but who is my rock, my best friend and, yes, my *real* sister. And then there is the love that took over my very heart; the love I have for my children. I did not give birth to any of them, yet they are my love, my world, my heart, and my joy. There was never a moment that I looked at any of those three tiny beings and wondered if I could love them. Even on our most difficult of days, even on days when every button I had was pushed or no sleep had been had, I loved them. I love them now and will forever and ever and ever- amen!

Our children do not have to follow every rule we have for us to love them. They do not have to look or act exact as we do for us to love them. Our children do not have to be anywhere near perfect for us to sacrifice for them. We will catch vomit in our bare hands, take a third job to put them through college, stand in front of a bus, fight an angry mountain lion and give them every ounce of ourselves. I think that is when we are living most in God's image, when we give to people that we do not expect anything back from. When we give and love merely because these messy, fussy, creative, funny, imperfect little people are our children. Doesn't God do the same for us?

I am so thankful that God loves me merely because I am His child. I am thankful that my parents did the same and that I too have been given the opportunity to give my love unconditionally, purely and in every way to these children who have blessed my world just by being here. God truly does pour love around you. Take it in.

If you are in the process of adopting, no matter whether you are in a good place with your journey or you are impatient, wondering when your child will come, focus on 1 John. Let yourself feel God's love and be renewed. Look at how you are changing and your own heart has grown five sizes. If you already have your sweet lil' people at home you know what I am talking about- even on your worst day. Love. Unwavering, stubborn, warm, fierce and forever. Love. You get that first from God and you have had it since your name first passed His lips. He has known you and loved you since before you were born. Sound familiar?

With lots of ♥ & gratitude for the love I have known,
Madeleine

Do you believe God loves you unconditionally?
Who do you feel loved by in your life?
Who do you love with every fiber of your being (the kind of love that would make you fight an angry bear or jump out in front of a bus, kind off love)?

29

PATIENCE

"But if we hope for what we do not see, we wait for it with patience."
Romans 8:25

I love to walk on the beach. It reminds me of my grandmother and seeing her collect shells at the family beach house we visited each summer. I would watch her tiny frame, leaning down to pick up each one. She had so much patience. She would sift through seemingly endless grains of sand to find the tiniest of shark's teeth, yet when I looked, I found none. I knew they were there because she had huge glass lamp bases that were filled with them. A sea of black and gray. She found so many because she was patient, she enjoyed the process and took her time. I was always in a hurry. I wanted things right now and became quickly discouraged and frustrated when I could not find the sharks teeth right away. I did not enjoy the process of searching and waiting, which made it seem all the longer. I gave up easily and did not reap a reward. (Galatians 6:9)

The adoption process began much the same way for me. Though I was excited and zoomed through my home study and fingerprints and interviews, nothing could happen fast enough. I had control over very little and quickly became frustrated and impatient. I had done all I could. I waited. I prayed. Patience is and never has been one of my virtues. As a hopeful parent, I felt like a child again, scooping the sand with both hands, hurriedly throwing it to the side, no shark's tooth in sight. In my impatience I was no longer enjoying the process, the journey that would bring me to my child.

The same can be said in motherhood. Tantrums at meal time. Your family room covered in toys and sippy cups. Morning arguments over outfits that rival Rainbow Brite's. Running lil' folks to sports and art class and a friend's house. The peanut free/gluten free/ food dye free cupcakes you have to come up with for the class party. The "disguise a turkey" project you have to help finish that your child told you about the night before it's due. We prayed for this, right? We wanted parenthood. How quickly we lose patience. How quickly the day to day process takes over and we can no longer enjoy the journey.

Hang on! You have this. Be patient with yourself. Be patient with your children and the journey. Romans 12:12 says to ""Rejoice in hope, be patient in tribulation, be constant in prayer." I know being patient when times are tough is easier said than done, but this part will not last forever. Don't hurry it. Today may be a part of your journey to your child. It may be another day to tell your child you love them. These are the days. We cannot wait for some imaginary, perfect day, and we shouldn't rush all the days in-between. Take it in. Embrace it. These are the days you may wish you could go back to.

With ♥ and hopes your shark's tooth is right there in front of you,
Madeleine

What do you have the least patience for?
What can you do to change the situation?
Have you prayed about it?

30

PEACE

"Turn away from evil and do good; seek peace and pursue it."
Psalm 34:14

From the outside, adoption seems to be many things: taboo, phenomenal, incredible, beautiful, interesting. But when you are in the trenches, you quickly discover that adoption is a journey that requires you to make a lot of decisions. Many of these decisions can change the trajectory of another person's life.

Will you adopt internationally, domestically, or through foster care? Do you wish to select the sex, gender, race, and ability of your future child? Are you open to adopting twins? What about a sibling group? How do you feel about contact with the child's biological family? How much money can you spend on an adoption? Are you will to accept a legally risky situation? Are you willing to pay expectant or birth parent living expenses? Which lawyer or agency will you use?

The choices an adoptive parent are required to make is daunting. Saying yes to something is saying no to something else. Saying no makes you question your faith. And sometimes decisions must be made immediately, without time to take a deep breath, ask a lot of questions, or spend quiet time seeking God's voice.

There were several times over the course of the past seven years when we would get a call from our attorney or social worker asking if we'd like to be considered for a particular adoption situation. Each time my heart would pound furiously and I would begin to think of a million what ifs. I would sometimes call one of my nurse friends to ask about a medical condition or furiously text a fellow adoptive mama for an opinion. Ultimately, the only times I felt as though a hand was resting on my shoulder and a voice was soothingly and reassuringly telling me things would be ok, was when I took the situation to God in prayer. Though the outcome wasn't always what I hoped, the gift of peace was bestowed upon me, as promised, when I pursued it.

When it comes to making tough decisions, our mission is clear: we have to turn away from evil, those times when God clearly tells us to say no or when a decision presented to us goes against what we know to be right, true, and just. Instead, we have to choose to do good. We have to "seek peace" and when God gives us the answer we beckon Him for, we have to obey and pursue the peace He has granted us. Peace never just falls into our laps. It's a choice.

Pursuing peace,
Rachel

What adoption related situation or decision is causing you to feel restless today?
How can you pursue peace, even in the midst of confusion or chaos?

31

PRAYER

"Continue steadfastly in prayer, being watchful in it with
thanksgiving;"
Colossians 4:2

Prayer has always been my lifeline. When there were moments
when I felt all options were gone, prayer showed me that was
not true. The hardest part about praying is knowing that as
humans, our plan is not always His plan. It is a difficult thing to rec-
oncile when we feel strongly that something is right for us, that HE
may have different plans.

I did a lot of praying when my sweet mommy was diagnosed with
cancer. She was my rock here on Earth, the woman who had built my
faith in the Lord was being attacked by this awful disease. There was
no question that every waking hour I was "praying without ceasing"
(1 Thessalonians 5:17). Praying for her to be healed. Praying for that
miracle that the next scan would show the tumor gone. Praying that I
would give her a grandchild. NOW. Those were my plans. My hopes.
My prayers.

It was not to be. The miracle of healing was not part of my mom's
story here on Earth. I did not become pregnant or adopt before my
sweet mommy went on to be with the Lord. It was so hard to see then,

in the midst of her illness that having a child would have kept me from that precious time with her: being near her on the rides to her medical appointments and the long conversations while she rested on her bed.

My sweet first baby came to me through adoption just fifty-one weeks after my mother's death. What a blessing he was to all of my family for so many reasons. He brought us joy on that difficult first anniversary of losing mom. God knew. His plan is always greater than ours, even when we do not see it.

I have learned to pray differently now. I now pray that His will be done for the best of those involved. Praying this way was something that truly helped me, as we travelled our subsequent adoption journey. Trust in God. Hand your worries to Him through prayer and He will do what is best for you. To pray that His will be done is to know that what comes next is the best for you whether you understand His plan or not and no matter what part of your life you are speaking to him about. God is always listening. HE LOVES YOU. HE KNOWS EVERY HAIR ON YOUR HEAD. He has even numbered them! (Luke 12:7) I am ever humbled in knowing my worth to Him and it allows me to speak to HIM about everything on my heart, knowing he wants what is best for me. HE wants what is best for you too, talk to HIM.

The Bible says, more times than I am going to count, to "look up". It is good advice, no matter what the situation to "look up" for answers always. Pray. Talk to your Father in Heaven. He wants to hear from you and you will feel better for it. Do not look out for answers in this world. There is only one true direction and that is Him.

With ♥ & ceaseless prayer-
Madeleine

How have you been praying?
Are you having trouble accepting that HIS will, whether we understand it or not, is what is best for you?
What have you been praying ?

32

PREPAREDNESS

"Let not your hearts be troubled. Believe in God; believe also in
me. In my Father's house are many rooms. If it were not so, would
I have told you that I go to prepare a place for you? And if I go
and prepare a place for you, I will come again and will take you to
myself, that where I am you may be also. And you know the way to
where I am going."
John 14:1-4

I am a list maker. I find great joy in making a big ol' long list and checking each thing off as I make my way through the day. I am a person who likes to put things on the calendar ahead of time and color code it if I can, then when that week comes, all important information is transcribed to the chalkboard in the kitchen for immediate viewing. I am a gal who loves to welcome overnight guests with a bathroom full of anything they might need or may have forgotten. Soap? Deodorant? Tooth brushes and floss? Q-tips? You need it? I have it! I like to be prepared. I can't help it, I come from a family like that. My sweet grandmother had a big jug of sweet tea on stand-by in her refrigerator and always pulled something scrumptious from the big chest freezer if unexpected company arrived. She was so prepared. Not just her freezer, but her heart. She did not care what time of day someone came or if it were dinner time. She would just add another name to the pot and put out another set of silverware, genuinely happy to have another place set at the table.

Knowing there are people on this planet that love you enough to prepare for you, who are honestly happy just to be in your company is a special thing. Even more special is the way God and Jesus have prepared for us. What a humbling thing to know.

Our precious Jesus was sent to this earth to save us from our sins because we had been chosen by God. Jesus then left this earth for us to prepare a seat for us in the Kingdom of Heaven. Do not let the enormity of this be lost on you. God knows you. God loves you. You are His child and He wants to be with you. You always have a place to go when you have God. You and your hopes for a child and a loving family are not forgotten. Your prayers to be the parent your child needs are heard. God knows your heart.

If He has a place prepared for you in Heaven, then of course he has a plan for you and has provided for you on Earth.

With ♥ and sweet tea,
Madeleine

How have you prepared your heart, your table, your life, your home for the child you will welcome?
What can you do to better prepare a place for God in your life?
Have you accepted that God is just happy to be with you? That God loves you for you?
Have you prepared your child for this world by giving them the gift of faith and loving affirmations that reinforce it?
God is preparing for YOU! What are you preparing for?

33

PRIDE

"When pride comes, then comes disgrace,
but with the humble is wisdom."
Proverbs 11:2

Choosing to build your family through adoption means at times you will naturally feel isolated. Your family will experience situations and emotions that are unique. You may find that you distance yourself from friends and family (and likewise, they might distance themselves from you) or members of your child's racial community as you face particular challenges. When this happens, you may build up some resentment, anger, hurt, and confusion. And in response, you may be inclined to choose pride.

The problem with pride is that it encourages self-reliance. *I can handle this myself!* And perhaps, in some ways, you can. After all, you know your child best. However, what happens when you do need help, yet you refuse to ask for it? The Bible assures us that pride results in disgrace. On the contrary, humbleness results in wisdom.

I recall a time when my husband and I were shopping for a greeting card. We had our eight- month-old daughter, our first child, strapped into the cart. Two African American women approached us and said, "Your baby's hair is dry." I felt my face flush with simultaneous anger and embarrassment. "Come with us," the women said, as they started off down the aisle. We hesitated for a moment and then, out of curiosity, surrendered. We spent the next thirty minutes listening to the ladies' hair and skin care advice as they showed us product after product. Then one of the ladies said, "We don't care what race you are. We just want to help you with your baby's hair."

There have been many times throughout our parenting journey where someone has helped us, solicited or not. Their advice, encouragement, and support has been incredibly beneficial to our family. Had I chosen to dig my heels in and refuse, embracing pride over humbleness, we wouldn't be the parents we are today. Humbleness has given us, as the Bible promises, wisdom.

With humbleness,
Rachel

In what ways have you resisted support and advice from family, friends, adoption professionals, birth parents, adoptees, or even strangers? What areas of adoptive parenting do you need support with right now?

34

REASSURANCE

"For the righteous will never be moved; he will be remembered forever. He is not afraid of bad news; his heart is firm, trusting in the LORD. His heart is steady; he will not be afraid, until he looks in triumph on his adversaries."

Psalm 112:6-8

Two of my three children went off to pre-school without any tears (I, on the other hand was a hot mess when they left). It was the last one. It was my baby of the three- the fiercest, seemingly most fearless one of the bunch, who was the white knuckled crier. He would scream, "I just want to give you a hug", and chase me down the hallway when I would drop him off. It broke my heart. I already didn't want my baby leaving home, but I knew I had to walk him back to his teacher. I gently told him in all his boo-boo faced glory that I would be back and I loved him. I gave him a kiss on his hand, leaving a lipstick mark and told him I was with him even when he couldn't see me. When I got around the corner I would snuggle up to the wall where I could not be seen and wait to hear that his crying stopped. Then I went to the van and sometimes cried, myself. I knew he had to stay and learn that he was strong. Each day when I picked him up he would run to me, happy as a clam and say, "I knew you were coming!"

"...I will never leave you nor forsake you." (Hebrews 13:5)

Sometimes things are tough. Sometimes we do not know where life or even today is taking us. We are not promised rainbows and lollipops every day. We are not promised long beach walks and peaceful moments with family. Life can be a struggle. It is fraught with trials and even when we know they are there to make us stronger it is still hard sometimes. You know how you ask your spouse or best bud if your rear end looks fat in your jeans? You don't do it because you hope they say "yes" if it does, you do it for reassurance before you step out in to the world. We all need some reassurance when we step out into the world. God is that reassurance.

I wish we could all walk around with a kiss print on our hand and remember that God is there even when it seems as though you are alone. I hope that for this moment I can be your reassurance that things will be o.k.. I have been that white knuckled crier, too. The adoption journey at times can make you feel very alone. The journey to adopt does not go on forever, it just feels like it - so try to enjoy what you can, this is your path to your child. Things are always changing and that can be scary, for preschoolers and grown-ups but we have to grab onto the journey and know He is there.

Tiny ones going through withdrawal or just needing care won't always be fussy- embrace that they need the extra snuggles, one day they will be too busy. You won't always be exhausted- one day these little people will grow up and you will wish someone was calling you from their bed. Homework seems to never end, but one day it will and your afternoon will not be filled with the chatter of little voices. You will go from being a parent, to being a tired parent, a proud parent, a parent who questions every decision you make to being a parent of grown children. It goes just that fast and all along HE will be there, even though you may not see Him.

You see, He is our parent, too and he will always heed our call, for that you can rest assured. Like I left a kiss print on my children's hands to remind them I was there with them, God left his mark on our hearts and his promise was made in the blood off His son Jesus. There is no greater promise or reassurance on this Earth and on this day than that! Just as I reminded my sweet lil guy that I was always there with him- God is always with you. He wants you to see how strong YOU are, but he is never far away. KNOW that.

With ♥ & a giant kiss print,
Madeleine
P.S. If your little one is headed off to school, *The Kissing Hand* by Audrey Penn is a WONDERFUL book we loved so much (about the fears of starting school).

How do you find reassurance from God?
When do you feel the furthest from Him? When do you feel the closest to Him?
What reminders can you find that He is never far away?

35

REFUGE

God is our refuge and strength, a very present help in trouble.
Psalm 46:1

I've been guilty of running to anyone and anything but God when I'm feeling angry, restless, confused, or hurt, particularly when it comes to adoption-related issues. I'll vent to my husband, text a friend, call my sister, ask for opinions on a Facebook group. I'll allow my feelings to dictate my mood for the day. I feel like a frantic, discombobulated, anxious mess inside, and I choose to allow these emotions to ooze out, affecting those around me. This happens, in particular, when things do not go according to my carefully laid plans or my unrealistic expectations are not met. Adoption and parenting, as you probably realize, is unpredictable, ever-changing, and full of surprises that aren't always pleasant or anticipated.

Psalm 46:1 reminds us that God is "our refuge and strength." He's right beside us, waiting for us to recognize who He is and what He is capable of. He's also "a very present help." He's not distant, apathetic, or cold (unlike how many people can be when we are facing tough circumstances and raw feelings). He wants and loves the real you: authentic and messy.

Take, for example, when you run into an acquaintance at the grocery store or are sitting by a co-worker. Usually the conversation goes like this. One person says, "How are you?" The other person mutters, "Fine," and might even display a fake smile (to be more convincing). If he or she is feeling particularly polite that day, it will be followed up by, "How are you?" This basic exchange is meant to be friendly enough, but most of us don't want the other to share how he or she is *really* doing that day.

God, on the other hand, can handle our big feelings. He's is Refuge. He is Strength. He's not just "present," but "very present" in our times of trouble. Though support systems are invaluable gifts from God, they are not a replacement for the Prince of Peace.

Relishing in refuge,
Rachel

What BIG feelings are you dealing with today?
Who do you usually turn to first when life gets messy?

36

RELEASE

"casting all your anxieties on him, because he cares for you."
1 Peter 5:7

It's stuck in our heads for seemingly forevermore: the song *Let It Go*. The reason the song is so popular, besides the fact that it was produced by Disney, is that the words empower its listeners. We *want* to let it go, whatever our "it" is, but it's scary. To let go of control (though often a false sense), of burdens, of unproductive grudges, of someone else's transgressions (or your own), means opening up oneself to vulnerability. But we are tempted. How cool would it be to dance in the snow, throwing off our cape and letting down our proverbial hair, while singing into the starry sky about how free we finally are?

The thing is, casting our cares into a sky isn't going to heal us. We may temporarily feel better, but the things we are worrying about, the things we are tormented over, will come back to haunt us. The only true way to release the things we are inwardly battling is to cast our anxieties "on Him." Why? Because He cares for us: deeply, without excuse or condition. He created us. He loves us. He died for us. He's crazy about us.

There are many things that happen along the adoption and parenting journey that can be incredibly daunting, confusing, and frustrating. There are things that will happen that make zero sense, things you didn't desire or anticipate. Once you have a child or children in your family, there will be challenges that stem from adoption, or the fact that your family looks different from other families. There might be resistant family members and friends. You might struggle with adapting to your child's physical or emotional needs.

You want sweet release, but you aren't sure you are ready. What if God doesn't like what He sees? What if He doesn't deliver on His promises? What if everything really isn't going to be ok? In these times of trial, you have two choices: continue to hang on and just hope for your snowy night or cast "all your anxieties on him, because he cares for you."

Casting daily,
Rachel

What are your greatest sources of anxiety right now?
What are the pros of releasing your anxieties to God versus trying to control and handle the situations yourself?

37

RESPONSIBILITY

"You shall love the LORD your God with all your heart and with all
your soul and with all your might. And these words that I command
you today shall be on your heart. You shall teach them diligently to
your children, and shall talk of them when you sit in your house,
and when you walk by the way, and when you lie down, and when
you rise. You shall bind them as a sign on your hand, and they shall
be as frontlets between your eyes."
Deuteronomy 6:5-8

As parents we have so many responsibilities. Sometimes I can
hardly believe I am "The Grown Up," much less "The Mom."
How did that happen!?! I am the cook, the seamstress, the
taxi driver, the coach, the cheerleader, the teacher, the playmate, the
schedule maker, The Tooth Fairy and a thousand other things. So
many parts go into being the parent. So many responsibilities are on
a parents' job description. For any other job, it would not be worth it!
We are preparing children for the big world! As if that is not enough,
some parents are also navigating fully open adoptions, transracial
adoption and parenting children of trauma. Add to all of that, an-
swering our children's random questions about adoption while navigating the household aisle at Target. It is our responsibility to answer

those questions our children have honestly, age appropriately and without judgment. It is for us to guide them in any further search for themselves or anything else. And it is for us to give them the greatest gift that a parent can give their child, the greatest gift my mother gave me, faith.

Sharing your faith with your child is not only a good thing to do, it is an amazing gift that will guide this now small person through to adulthood. It is also what God has commanded. God does not give a ton of instructions about parenting. It would probably would be easier if God had included a handbook with each newborn regarding his or her care. What God does give clear instruction about is sharing faith. In Deuteronomy 6, Moses comes right out and says that God expects us to pass down the lessons of faith from one generation to the next and to show it throughout our daily life. Whether you are driving and someone cuts you off, you are at the store, tucking the kids into bed, making dinner, or doing leg lifts, God wants you to be teaching your child faith. That means you have to have some faith AND choose to LIVE IT! Children truly live by example. Your example of faith will help your child stay strong in times of trouble. Your example will affect how your child treats other people. And the love your child feels you have for them and for God, will help them through every day they spend here on this earth.

There is nothing in the Bible about when a baby should roll over, if I am a failure because I did not breastfeed or stating we should buy our kids a car when they turn sixteen, but what is repeated on more than one occasion is sharing our faith:

"Train up a child in the way he should go: and when he is old, he
will not depart from it." (Proverbs 22:6)
"Command these things as well, so that they may be without
reproach. But if anyone does not provide for his relatives, and
especially for members of his household, he has denied the faith
and is worse than an unbeliever." 1Timothy5: 7-8 "Fathers, do not
provoke your children to anger, but bring them up in the discipline
and instruction of the Lord." (Ephesians 6:4)

It is hard to be an example all of the time. Sometimes part of being the responsible example is reminding our kids we are human and we make mistakes. Those times can be teachable moments for grace, forgiveness and redemption. If you do this right, your child's faith will outlive you. If you are still waiting for your child, use this time to look at what a child would learn from your faithful life.

With ♥ & thankfulness that this part has instructions
Madeleine

Are you modeling a faithful life? How so?
What ways and opportunities can you use to teach a share a child about faith and its ability to move mountains?

38

RESTORATION

"For we are glad when we are weak and you are strong. Your
restoration is what we pray for."
2 Corinthians 13:9

A lot of non-believers I've talked to seem to think that they
can only come before God if and when they are a certain
something. This might mean stopping a particular behavior,
looking a different way, or thinking more "holy" thoughts. Even some
Christians feel this way, despite what the Bible promises. We think
that we have to "look the part" in order to approach God.

Newsflash: We ain't foolin' God.

I remember the incredibly dark days I had before I finally had an
answer to my concerning medical symptoms. I would curl up in my
bed and cry, asking God why the doctors couldn't figure out what was
wrong with me and why so many people made degrading, hateful
comments about ever-thinning body. I remember staring at my wedding picture, framed beautifully and sitting on my nightstand, and
mourning the girl I once was. I was desperate. I was broken. One
minute I'd be cursing at God, and the next minute I would be crying
out to Him. A part of me held on to pride and a can-do attitude. *I
will figure this out,* I told myself, attempting to console my aching soul.

Looking back, I was angry at God. He knew the answer, but He sure hadn't bestowed it upon me or the numerous medical professionals I had visited. I felt like I was part of some sick joke, like the target of a hidden camera television show.

What I learned from my pre-diagnosis days is that God was with me, carrying me, holding me, encouraging me. It came in the form of a song on the radio, a person who crossed my path, or something I would read in a devotional. Somehow, I kept fighting whatever was harming my body. And thankfully those little miracles and motivations to keep on happened, because the day I was diagnosed could have been my last day. But it wasn't. Restoration was brewing.

You likely have come to the place of choosing adoption because you've had days and seasons like mine. They aren't pretty. They are debilitating, life-sucking, depressing times. They aren't something you want to look back on. But they happened. Maybe they are still happening. And what I want you to know is that God's about to do something. And in the meantime, you rely on One who can provide the one thing you so desperately need: restoration.

Restored and pressing on,
Rachel

What is or has been your most desperate time?
What does restoration mean to you in your situation?

39

SELF-AWARENESS

"Examine yourselves, to see whether you are in the faith. Test yourselves. Or do you not realize this about yourselves, that Jesus Christ is in you?—unless indeed you fail to meet the test!"
2 Corinthians 13:5

I know a lot about myself. Sometimes I wish I didn't. I know I am a people pleaser and have been since I was a little girl. I would "surprise" my mom by cleaning the bathroom without being asked. I know I talk a lot and sometimes loudly. It's probably why my mom once asked me if my mouth was getting tired because her ears were. I know I have no patience with poor table manners. I will likely give you the eyebrow if you talk with your mouth full, and I can't stand noisy chewers. I know I cannot be trusted in a room alone with an almond Snickers bar. I know that I love with everything in me and struggle with understanding those who don't. I know I will cry every time I watch *The Notebook*. EVERY. SINGLE. TIME. I know that if driveway roller skating had been an Olympic event, I would be a Gold Medalist. I know I can easily forgive but never forget. In a nutshell. I am aware of who I am.

Knowing who you are and being aware of your capabilities and limitations is a very important part of the adoption process. The commitments you make to yourself, to the child, to birth family members, and to God are forever. We cannot take them lightly. There are so many things you have to consider when you set out on this journey. What kind of adoption are you comfortable with; domestic, international, foster? What health risks or exposures are you willing to accept? Are you open to children of ethnicities other than yours? What level of openness are you willing to share with the birth family? Would you open your home to a child who had experienced extensive trauma or who has special needs? These are tough questions and sometimes the answers are even harder to work through. You wonder what kind of person you are or Christian you are because you have not just flung your doors wide open to EVERY scenario. Don't. What is most important is that you are honest with yourself: about who you are and what you can handle. Everyone is not a match for every scenario. Keep in mind, what you felt you could take on with your first adoption may change with your second.

Being self-aware does not mean being critical of yourself; it means you are being honest with yourself, knowing where you can truly excel, what you need to work on,, and what is just a truth about yourself that is not likely to change. We are all finding our way in this world, doing the best that we can. Self-awareness and self-truth is a part of finding a way we can make a difference. Just because you did not feel you were suited for one adoption situation does not mean you are a bad person, that you have failed, or that you do not care- it means you were meant for something else. It means you can make a difference elsewhere.

Self-awareness is knowledge, important knowledge. Knowing who you are, where your talents lie, what your deficits are, what motivates you and what your deepest beliefs are can only serve to help you along your journey whether it is building your family, parenting, playing a role in your church family or any other endeavor. So dig deep, my friend. You know the answers. Do not be ashamed or afraid- be aware.

With ♥, roller skates, & almond Snickers crumbs,
Madeleine

Are you self-aware?
Can you clearly define your assets, deficits, motivations and beliefs?
How do God and your faith play a role in who you think you are?

40

SELF-WORTH

"Do you not know that you are God's temple and that
God's Spirit dwells in you?"
1 Corinthians 3:16
"For you formed my inward parts; you knitted me
together in my mother's womb."
Psalms 139:13

Sometimes I wonder if I am enough. Am I smart enough? Do I look good enough? Do I play with my children enough? Have I taught them enough of the right things? I will be honest, I should not be your first pick for a "phone a friend" if you are ever a contestant on *Who Wants to Be a Millionaire*. I will struggle with weight issues no matter what the scale says, likely for the rest of my life. I am the queen of kickball, but sometimes I tell the kids I can't play because I am making dinner. And though I try to cover my bases, I have not yet taught my daughter how to sew on a button, and my boys still put in another bite of food when they haven't finished the last. And yes, I gave up on a personal Pinterest account because it was too much pressure to accomplish all the crafts and projects I pinned.

I was not perfect when we began the adoption process either. I had less gray hair (though, this mama is not above coloring now), and I had a cleaner house, but I was not perfect. Just as I find myself doing now, I could be quick to de-value myself, to assign myself very little worth. I did not feel I had tons to offer children beyond my love. I wondered if an expectant mom would choose us. We were chosen, and all three times in less time than I could have carried any of our sweet babies, but still I questioned myself.

With three children at home I wondered if I was using the right bottle. Did they have enough tummy time? Was I potty training at the proper age? Should I push memorizing the alphabet more? There were too many questions that I felt like I did not know the answers to. Was I getting too pudgy eating whatever the children left on their plate and having no time to exercise? Was my husband bored talking to me because I was home with the kids all day and sometimes randomly started singing the *Dora the Explorer* song even after they were in bed? I felt like I was of very little good to anyone. What was my value?

Even now that my children are a little older I wonder- Should they have less homework and more time outside? Should I be giving them more chores to learn more responsibility? Am I doing this right? Will anyone read my article? I guess I am still kinda pudgy. There are days that I give and give and I feel like the stump of *The Giving Tree* but still don't feel like that is enough. Am I good enough for anyone? I have visited and revisited this question over my entire life but a few weeks ago, Pastor Todd told me something that stuck. He shared something with me that answered the question. He reminded me in his sermon that the Holy Spirit lives inside me! It is a game changing reminder. The Holy Spirit lives in me! What a gift it was to be reminded of that, right in that moment! The Holy Spirit lives inside YOU, too! I am going to give you a little second to let that sink in...

Did you forget? Did you ever really know or even think about it? THE HOLY SPIRIT LIVES IN YOU! (yes, that was me yelling it!) Now next time you listen to your negative inner dialogue or opinions of others remember this: the only opinion that really matters is that of God and Jesus and they thought you valuable enough that Jesus died on the cross for you! FOR YOU! We are worth it. We are enough. How could we not be with the Holy Spirit living inside of us? When Jesus died for us?

So be kind to yourself today. It doesn't matter if your Pinterest account has 400 pins of projects you will never do or if you sing the *Doc McStuffins* theme song when you are alone in the car! Know that you can do great things and that you are valuable. Your self-worth does not rest on whether you are chosen now or later or what rating you would give yourself as a parent. No, you are worthy because you are His.

With ♥ and God as my "lifeline"-
Madeleine

Instead of regular questions with this devotional, I want to encourage you to do what Pastor Todd did with the congregation. We were all given a rubber band and encouraged to write "H.S." on it and wear it for a week as a reminder that the Holy Spirit lives inside of each of us. I wish I could give you a rubber band right now, but I encourage you to do this on your own. You will be amazed at how differently you feel every day as you remind yourself that the Holy Spirit is in you. You can do better and be stronger because the Holy Spirit is in you and you are enough because YOU, yourself, your body are a temple of God. He dwells in you!

How does the reminder that you are worth it and that the Holy Spirit lives in you, make you feel?

41

SERENITY

"Peace I leave with you; my peace I give to you.
Not as the world gives do I give to you. Let not your hearts be
troubled, neither let them be afraid."
John 14:27
"But the wisdom from above is first pure, then peaceable,
gentle, open to reason, full of mercy and good fruits,
impartial and sincere."
James 3:17
"fear not, for I am with you; be not dismayed, for I am your God;
I will strengthen you, I will help you, I will uphold you with my
righteous right hand."
Isaiah 41:10

I am a worrier. I have spent a ton of my life worrying about just about everything, whether I could do anything about it or not. Don't get me wrong, I prayed about my concerns but never really handed it over, accepting the true peace and serenity that Jesus offers. I spent years stealing my own joy by banging my head against the wall, worrying about things I could not change on my own. What? I was in a lull from worrying about my husband and kids? I'd worry about yours. I have been a hand wringer. I could have rubbed a hole in a worry stone when I should have been relying on the true Rock.

I should have known how hard being the grown up would be. My own mama had the Serenity Prayer propped in her kitchen windowsill where she could see it every day. She could have been the poster child for faith. She was a strong, "optimistic-realist" but still she needed the reminder of peace, courage and wisdom that the serenity prayer brings.

God, grant me the serenity to accept the things I cannot change,
The courage to change the things I can,
And the wisdom to know the difference.

I wish when the prayer was shared that more often it included the full version. Often times the 2nd half, is left off. This is one of the most important parts. It's the part that reminds you to hand it over to God. Of the importance of His will being done and the greater picture of things when you consider eternity:

Living one day at a time;
Enjoying one moment at a time; Accepting hardships as the pathway to peace;
Taking, as He did, this sinful world as it is, not as I would have it;
Trusting that He will make all things right if I surrender to His Will;
That I may be reasonably happy in this life and supremely happy with
Him Forever in the next.
Amen

When I think of serenity, I think of Psalm 23, "He makes me lie down in green pastures. He leads me beside still waters He leads me beside still waters. He restores my soul" (Psalm 23:2-3) and of my great-grandmother. When I visited her from childhood on through college there was always a routine followed at bedtime. After putting on pajamas and brushing our teeth we would lay on her bed and she would let me read aloud from *Guideposts* or *The Upper Room*, we would do leg lifts (even when she was ninety-years-old!) and then say prayers and the 23rd Psalm together. She was a woman of amazing strength and faith. She had survived the depression, the death of two sons before their time and two husbands, one of whom died when her children were just boys. She kept the family pharmacy afloat until she could get my grandfather through college to take over and as a widow, ran a tourist home. There was nothing she could not do because she had the attitude that, you do what you can. You do what has to be done. Serenity. There was no time for worry. There was no time for wavering faith. She took hold of whatever she could change and the rest she handed to God, all the while her hair was perfectly done, and wearing pearl earrings and a belted dress. I can't seem to do it some days in yoga pants and a ponytail!

For some reason we seem to think it is easier to worry and fret than it is to hand our worries, fears and pains all over to God. I worried and fretted through our first adoption while my husband was calm in his faith. What a difference there is in our experiences when we hand over what is not ours to change! We cannot change if an expectant parent is going to decide to parent rather than place. We cannot change if a country cuts off adoptions or if we are made to wait. We cannot change the circumstances that our children faced before coming to us. We have to decide what it is we can change, and sometimes that is ourselves. Hand some of the things you cannot change over to God today and let His peace and serene walk by the still waters bring you peace. (Yoga pants and pearl earrings optional.)

With ♥ and leg lifts,
Madeleine

Are you a worrier?
What do you spend the most time worrying about? Are these things you could do anything about?
Can you hand them over to God? What kind of difference would that make in your daily life?
Have you found that combination of peace, wisdom and courage that can only come from Him?

42

STRENGTH

"but they who wait for the Lord shall renew their strength; they shall
mount up with wings like eagles; they shall run and not be weary;
they shall walk and not faint."
Isaiah 40:31

A doption is not for the faint at heart. First, the journey will
never go as you hope for or plan. There will always be delays,
changes, and challenges. You will feel like you are being tested while you are waiting for your child. Second, after placement is
when much of the hard work begins, and parenting, well, it's forever.

How is it possible to be strong in the face of difficulty, confusion, and uncertainty? What happens if the expectant mother you
are matched with decides to parent? What happens when you realize
you are $10,000 short of the money you need to adopt a child from
China? What happens if, for the fourth time, you aren't selected to
adopt a particular child from foster care? What about if your spouse
decides that he isn't ready to adopt at this time?

There have been many times over the course of our adopting
and parenting journey where I felt that all my strength was gone.
When we weren't chosen by expectant parents, yet again, while we
waited for our first child. When, every single Sunday at church, at

least two people asked us if we had any adoption news to share. When we filled out the mountains of paperwork for a second and then third adoption. When our children asked us hard adoption questions that brought loss to the surface in full force.

The book of Isaiah offers us this truth: if we wait on God, our strength will be renewed. And not just renewed, but strongly renewed. We will soar and run. We will be able to endure anything that comes our way. Strength is contingent on our ability to rely on God and not on ourselves, because we will let ourselves down every single time.

The beauty of this verse is its lack of fine print. There is no gimmick, no false hope, no uncertainty. If we wait for God, we will gain exactly what we need: strength for the next step, the next season, the next journey. There is nothing God cannot do. And we can do everything by simply waiting on God and accepting the promise of strength.

In His mighty strength,
Rachel

What area of your adoption or parenting journey is causing you to feel weak?
In what ways has God encouraged you recently, providing you with the strength you need to take the next step, no matter how big or small?

43

STRUGGLE

"But he said to me, 'My grace is sufficient for you, for my power is made perfect in weakness.' Therefore I will boast all the more gladly of my weaknesses, so that the power of Christ may rest upon me. For the sake of Christ, then, I am content with weaknesses, insults, hardships, persecutions, and calamities. For when I am weak, then I am strong."
2 Corinthians 12:9-10

I am going to share something with you that usually only the cars stopped beside mine, know. When Carrie Underwood's version of *Jesus, Take the Wheel* comes on the radio; I immediately turn the volume waaaay up. As a matter of fact, the only thing louder than the radio is me. I cannot help but match Carrie word-for-word and with no less feeling (although some of her talent is missing from my version).

Sometimes the song brings me to tears. I know so well the ache of wanting to be on the right road but not knowing which way to go. I also know the sweet relief that has come in letting God get me where I need to be and the struggle that comes in-between. Why do we hold so tight to that wheel?

There have been times in my life that I felt God sent people into my life to get me back on the right path. Sometimes I felt as though God was working against me as he answered, "no" or redirected me at my every turn. When would my child come? Why was that so hard? Am I being the mother my children need me to be? Have I made the right choices for my children, where my work is concerned? These things that I have struggled with have all been softened and have been made better when I took my hands off the wheel and gave God the control in my life. He has driven me through more struggles than I care to mention.

When everything seems wrong and you are at your wits end- when you are tired- when you feel so very alone- grab your Bible, cry out to God for his help. Never be ashamed to ask God to take the wheel. He will drive you, He will carry you, He will get you where you need to be.

Now, go listen to JESUS TAKE THE WHEEL and belt it out loud- you will feel better!

With ♥ & loud singing-
Madeleine

Can you think of a time you have let God take the wheel?
What could you hand over to God, right now?
Do you continue to hold on to some things? What is keeping you from letting God take the wheel?

44

SURRENDER

"Do not be conformed to this world, but be transformed by the renewal of your mind, that by testing you may discern what is the will of God, what is good and acceptable and perfect."
Romans 12:2

I always looked forward to the day that I could work on fun school projects with my children. I had great memories of my mom helping me with my science projects and shoebox dioramas in grade school. What I have found as my own children go through their own elementary years is that it is really hard! Not the helping, but the standing by while they create their vision. I have had to surrender to the process and not grab the felt out of their hand and put it where it made sense to me. But my plan is not what is important here, no matter how amazing I am with the glue gun. It is not about what I think is best.

Having to give my glue gun skills a rest is much like our surrendering to God and His plans for us. While we have many skills and no doubt many plans for ourselves and our lives, it is His plan that is truly important. When there are issues in our life and we do not know which way to go we are not alone. We are not without direction. We must surrender ourselves to God's plan, as much as we do not understand it sometimes.

Even Jesus, sweet, sinless, Son of God, surrendered to his Father's plans. Plans that for Him, meant His own death for our sins. Jesus spoke to God about His plans not once, but three times in the Garden of Gethsemane in Matthew 26:39-44, "And going a little farther he fell on his face and prayed, saying, 'My Father, if it be possible, let this cup pass from me; nevertheless, not as I will, but as you will.'... Again, for the second time, he went away and prayed, 'My Father, if this cannot pass unless I drink it, your will be done.' And again he came and found them sleeping, for their eyes were heavy. So, leaving them again, he went away and prayed for the third time, saying the same words again."

God does not ask for that level of sacrifice from us, only that we stand strong in our faith in Him and give way for His Plans. Our God can move mountains, but we need to be available to surrender to the experience of watching. That may mean that our family building plans have involved more for us than most. It may mean we are not where we thought we would be on our personal journey right now. It might mean we have family struggles on a daily basis. It is sometimes the hardest thing in life not to fight His plan for us.

"For my thoughts are not your thoughts, neither are your ways my ways, declares the LORD" (Isaiah 55:8). The Lord's words are so true. We know that things do not always happen when we had planned for them to, as a matter of fact, more often than not- they don't happen then at all. We need to stop fighting, manipulating and trying to have our way. We have to toss our agenda out the window with the glue gun and surrender to his most perfect plan.

With ♥ and prayers for patience and surrender-
Madeleine

In what ways could you surrender yourself to God right now?
What parts of your adoption or parenting journey are you holding on to, parts you are afraid to surrender to Him?
Are you afraid that God's plan is different than yours?

45

TRANSFORMATION

"And do not be conformed to this world, but be transformed by the renewing of your mind, so that you may prove what the will of God is, that which is good and acceptable and perfect."
Romans 12:22

When I look back at who I was eight years ago when we started our adoption journey and who I am today, I'm thankful for the many ways I have been transformed. Transformation is the result of maturity, growth, applied knowledge, and change.

Eight years ago, I had no idea how to care for and style Black hair. Eight years ago, I didn't have the racial literacy to talk to my children about racism. Eight years ago, I didn't fully understand how beneficial open adoption could be. Eight years ago, I didn't grasp attachment parenting, correcting versus discipline, and the importance of valuing nature *and* nurture.

Transformation is an incredible opportunity that every adoptive parent has; however, too few have the courage to embrace it. To allow God to use situations and people to move us from point A to point B requires a personal willingness to "live and learn." Learning can be painful, uncomfortable, humbling, and demanding. In essence, transformation isn't easy.

When you choose to adopt, you choose to embark on a journey that encourages change in order for all family members to succeed and flourish. Transformation says "yes" to the bigger and better things that lie ahead. Transformation says "yes" to adoptees being free to be themselves, to express their feelings and opinions and give voice to their past experiences. Transformation says "yes" to adoptive parents being honest about challenges and joys.

The alternative to transformation is conformation. The Romans 12:22 warns us that conforming to "this world" rather than being "transformed by the renewing of your mind," isn't what God wants for us, nor is it what is best for us.

In essence, transformation says "yes" to God's hope for each of us: to being open to God's will, "that which is good and acceptable and perfect."

Saying yes,
Rachel

What is going on in your life that is asking you to choose between conformation and transformation?
What are the benefits to choosing transformation?

46

TRUTHFULNESS

"and then you will know the truth, and the truth will set you free."
John 8:32

Truth and freedom. They go hand-in-hand. One doesn't exist without the other. Knowing truth, sharing truth, and living in truth can be life-changing. Likewise, knowing truth but not living in it or sharing it can be devastating.

We often hear the phrase, "Be true to yourself." Certainly, being truthful with oneself and one's spouse, particularly during the adoption journey and after placement, is crucial to the family's well-being. Additionally, it's important to be truthful with the child you adopt. Though the truth can hurt (and in adoption, the circumstances of a placement are often very hard to hear, ponder, and accept), deception is more hurtful. Deception creates distrust which is detrimental to the parent-child relationship.

Over the course of your parenting journey, your child will demand answers from you. *Why was I placed for adoption? Why did you adopt? Where are my birth parents? Who are my birth parents? Why can't I see them? Why did they parent my birth brother but not me? Can I try to find them?* You may not have complete answers for your children, but you can give them the information that you do have, with full disclosure and empathy.

One of my children is much more interested in adoption than her siblings. One day she asked me, again, why she couldn't see one of her biological relatives. With her sitting on my lap facing me, I shared with her that unfortunately, despite our best efforts, the relative has chosen not to meet with us at this time. I then offered empathy: "That's really sad, isn't it?" We shared a long embrace, my eyes filled with tears, tears of both relief (for being honest) and empathy (for my child's hurting heart).

Truth starts with you. Before adopting, while adopting, after adopting, it's essential to do a lot of soul-searching, to be honest with yourself about your strengths and weaknesses, to admit when you are struggling with certain emotions and circumstances, and to face these things head-on so that you may cope in a healthy way and move forward. In doing so, you are helping your children learn to do the same. For certain, the truth isn't always pretty, but it is freedom-giving.

In freedom,
Rachel

What truths are you struggling with right now?
What can you do to effectively confront the truths so that you can be the best parent possible?

47

UNCERTAINTY

"Trust in the Lord with all your heart, and do not lean on your own understanding. In all your ways acknowledge him, and he will make straight your paths."
Proverbs 3:5-6

U ncertainty stems from that space between what we desire and feel and God's prompting. So what is a person to do when faced with uncertainty? Uncertainties like: *Should we pursue adoption at all? Should I submit my profile book for this potential adoption situation? Is it ok to specify the race or sex of the child we wish to adopt? Is pursuing a placement from the foster care system a good choice for our family? What if our adoption of a teenage boy doesn't work out? What if we aren't really prepared to adopt a child with special needs? Should we attempt infertility treatments one more time before moving on to adoption? What if I don't bond well with the child we adopt? How will my children react to their new sibling? How do I handle my family members and friends who are resistant to my decision to adopt?*

Adoption can be messy and complicated because there are humans involved, and humans are, from the very beginning of creation, tempted take actions that aren't in alignment with God's standards. Society encourages us to "follow our hearts"; however, our hearts can be incredibly deceiving at times, governed by emotions rather than godly principles.

You will be asked to make many choices throughout your adoption and parenting journey. Thinking about all of the choices at once can be overwhelming, even debilitating. Thus, confidence is easily shaken, and we readily forget that we stand on the Rock, not on sand.

We were never made to handle all of life's ups and downs alone. There is only one constant, one certainty, and that is God. He is the opposite of uncertainty. When you lay your next choice before Him, He will "make straight your paths."

Prayers for certainty,
Rachel

What is the next decision you need to make? What about this decision most concerns you?
What does Proverbs 3:5-6 promise you?

48

UNITY

"And though a man might prevail against one who is alone, two will withstand him—a threefold cord is not quickly broken."
Ecclesiastes 4:12

The foster child who, after being with you for over a year, is going home to his biological parents. The expectant mother you are matched with decides to parent her baby. The sibling pair you wanted to adopt has paperwork caught up in bureaucratic red tape. You aren't certain you can actually afford to adopt. The teenager you adopted two years ago is refusing to call you "mom." Your five-year-old son was just diagnosed with Reactive Attachment Disorder. Your daughter's birth mother is pregnant again, but is choosing to place the child with a different adoptive family.

Hardships in adoption are inevitable. There will be surprises, and they aren't always very pleasant. You will face circumstances that many of your family members and friends won't even begin to understand. You may feel quite isolated from the rest of the other parents in your community. The therapists and doctors you have enlisted to help your child aren't doing much helping.

In good and bad, it's incredibly important that you and your partner are unified. This isn't a time for a game of tug of war (no matter how frustrated and combative you feel). It's time to bind to-gether and remember you are on the same team. Though two might be able to "withstand" the challenges presented by adoption and parenting, a braid consisting of three strands, is "not quickly bro-ken." The ultimate strength comes from the unity created by three: the couple and God.

Certainly, this isn't easy to create or maintain. For one, parenting even one child can be an overwhelming task, particularly if that child has a traumatic past or has medical needs. For another, the child isn't the only responsibility of the couple. There are work responsibilities, the marital relationships, the household chores. There may be other stressors like an ailing family member, other children in the home, financial constrictions, personal health issues.

Ecclesiastes reminds us that the more strands we add to our rope, the stronger we are. And the three strands must start with the couple and God. Though perfection isn't promised, progress is.

Holding on to a three-strand rope,
Rachel

What challenges are you facing today that have you feeling scared, confused, frustrated, angry, or uncertain?
In what ways can you make your partner and God a priority in order to prevail against these challenges?

49

UNREST

"Come to me, all who labor and are heavy laden,
and I will give you rest."
Matthew 11:28

Seeking peace in all the wrong places is common when adopting. We desperately seek the next e-mail from our social worker, the next stamp of approval, the next stack of paperwork. We tell ourselves, *When X happens, then I will have peace.* But rest, as a result of peace, isn't found in any person, event, situation, or thing. True rest can only come from God, and it isn't contingent on anything here on Earth, including our ability to work hard and carry burdens on our own.

I'm naturally a bit of an anxious person. My type A personality thrives on control, order, and promptness: everything an adoption journey doesn't yield to or produce. Because I often held white-knuckled to false peace and attempt to be self-reliant, I was left feeling disappointed, confused, and conflicted. I have always had a difficult time surrendering control to God (or to anyone besides myself, really). However, there were times in our journey when I came face to face with the fact that God was the reliable rest-giver. Adoption is bittersweet, messy, and complicated. I will never find rest in it.

Society values and pushes us to always be hustling. Busyness is glorified. Parents boast of how tired they are from busing their children from one activity to the next, not having time to sit around a dinner table together. Bosses demand their employees work longer and longer hours. Exhaustion and anxiety make pharmaceutical companies rich.

Certainly, surrendering our tendencies to push harder and go longer isn't easy. But the relentless pursuit of physical, emotional, and spiritual exhaustion has dire consequences. Our children, or future children, need us to show them how to rest and rely on our heavenly Father, giving Him our stillness. It is during His gift of rest that we can listen, learn, reflect, and rejuvenate, so we can be prepared to face tomorrow.

Resting in His heavenly peace,
Rachel

What choices are you making that lead you to feel overwhelmed and exhausted?
From where are you currently seeking rest, well-knowing you will not receive it?

50

WEAKNESS

"My grace is sufficient for you, for my power is made perfect in
weakness."
2 Corinthians 12:9

Weakness is not something that is respected in society. We are supposed to be strong, resilient, and capable. We are supposed to make a way when there seemingly is no way. Hiding weakness is more popular than admitting, professing, dealing, and progressing.

But choosing to embark on an adoption journey, as well as parenting children from hard places, requires us to examine our weaknesses. When adopting and parenting, our future or current children can evoke things in us we thought we had buried or dealt with. We might be reminded of the loss of a child, the struggles with infertility, the times we weren't chosen. We might remember times we, like our children, also felt confused, afraid, angry, or hurt.

The good news is that weaknesses can serve a powerful purpose in our lives: they give us the opportunity to glorify God. One weakness all humans have is that we aren't capable of saving ourselves. We need Jesus' sacrifice on the cross in order to live an abundant life and have the promise of eternity with Him (Matthew 6:33; John 3:16).

Our weaknesses, rather great or seemingly small, are present to demonstrate God's grace, grace that is "sufficient," and to demonstrate that His "power is made perfect in weakness."

When things are going great, we often forget our need for a savior. And the beauty of our Savior is that He doesn't just save us once, but He steps in for us, granting us grace and strength, again, and again, and again. The most wonderful part of this verse is that His power becomes completely evident in the only thing we can really offer: our weaknesses.

In His power,
Rachel

What weaknesses are you wrestling with right now?
What does this verse promise us if we give God these weaknesses?

51

WISDOM

"If any of you lacks wisdom, let him ask God, who gives generously
to all without reproach, and it will be given him."
James 1:5
"But the wisdom from above is first pure, then peaceable,
gentle, open to reason, full of mercy and good fruits,
impartial and sincere."
James 3:17

When I think of those who have imparted wisdom on me I think of my grandmothers and their gentle spirits, amazing faith, and fierce love for God and their children. I think of my mother who showed me in every way that the love of a mother is forever. I think of the sweet older women in my churches (Miss Sallie Anne, her sister Peggy, Miss Jennie) who imparted wisdom over sweet potato pie. I think of the mothers I respect (both my peers and those who went before me), and the people at church and in my daily life that truly do their best to walk with God. I think of my Great Aunt Edith who was my mom's first example of a mother through adoption and is an living example of following God's word. Most times when I am unsure what I should do, which way I should turn or what path to take next I pray about it and ask

God for his wisdom. I also speak to those who have done so well in following His ways.

Sometimes with all the complicated issues involved in adoption it is easiest to be led only by our hearts. Of course we want to do what is right and what is right is not always what is easy. When it comes to issues of ethics in adoption, of after care for women who have placed, of how the termination of parental rights are handled, the promises that are made for the future and the handling of the heartbreak that is likely occurring on the other side, no doubt you will need wisdom, too.

Maybe you are wondering if now is really the right time to add to your family or if it feels okay to do an adoption fundraiser. Maybe you are thinking of adopting a second time or struggling with a relationship with a birth parent or one of your own family members. Ecclesiastes 8:5 says, "Whoever keeps a command will know no evil thing, and the wise heart will know the proper time and the just way." The truth is we do not always know what to do. We might know what we would like to do, but often need God's wisdom to truly know what is right.

The amazing thing is, you only need ask God and He will share His wisdom with you. Sometimes it comes in a whisper, and you truly have to be listening carefully for it. Other times it comes in a roar, and there is no doubting what you should do. Many times your answer can be found with prayer, in opening your Bible, or through the words of a trusted friend. "In all your ways acknowledge him, and he will make straight your paths." Proverbs 3:6

With ♥ as we find our way-
Madeleine

Who has God put in your path to help share his wisdom and navigate the path?
Do you listen for that still, soft voice? Do you follow it?
Share a time when you've heard God's roar. How does it feel to listen and obey, relishing in wisdom?

52

WORRY

"Therefore do not be anxious about tomorrow, for tomorrow will be anxious for itself. Sufficient for the day is its own trouble."
Matthew 6:34

I was a typical teenager: disrespectful, impatient, and certain I knew everything. I would roll my eyes at my mom, curse under my breath at my dad, and bad-mouth my teachers behind their backs. Meanwhile, these individuals would all be cheering for me, wanting the best for me, and worrying about me. And now that I'm a mom, I get it. There are so many worries to be mulled over for my children: their safety, their well-being, their future. There are immediate worries, short-term worries, and long-term worries.

I once read, "Worry is like a rocking chair. You rock and rock but never go anywhere." Worry happens rather naturally, but it is hardly productive. It encourages self-sufficiency, sadness, and fear. It discourages and cripples. Yet how should a Christian cope with worry when worry is an inevitable part of adoption and parenthood?

During this past year, I experienced a defining moment in our adoptive parenting journey. For quite a few months, one of my children had been experiencing fears and expressing questions related to her adoption story. I had struggled with how to respond to her, because the truth I needed to reveal to her wasn't pretty or easy. Until this point, my daughter had viewed her adoption as natural and positive. I was worried that revealing the truth to her would somehow hurt our relationship, darken her perception of her biological family, and shake her confidence.

On a sunny afternoon, she came to me, demanding answers. I remember drawing a breath and muttering a quick prayer for the right words. God granted my request and gave me in that moment my "daily bread" (Matthew 6:11). I was able to speak to my daughter with both honesty and empathy. Her response was not what I expected. Though she was sad, she also responded as if a weight had been lifted off her shoulders.

Friends, God gives us what we need "just in the nick of time." Worrying about tomorrow only ruins today. Worry steals joy and time. Worry gives power to the Enemy, but giving our concerns to God gives glory to Him.

With a less-anxious heart,
Rachel

What is your greatest worry today?
How does worry take away while faith adds to?

JOURNALING THE JOURNEY

♥

♥

♥

JOURNALING THE JOURNEY

♥

♥

♥

JOURNALING THE JOURNEY

♥

♥

JOURNALING THE JOURNEY

♥

♥

♥

JOURNALING THE JOURNEY

♥

♥

♥

♥

JOURNALING THE JOURNEY

♥

♥

♥

JOURNALING THE JOURNEY

♥

JOURNALING THE JOURNEY

♥

♥

RACHEL GARLINGHOUSE & MADELEINE MELCHER

♥

♥

JOURNALING THE JOURNEY

♥

♥

♥

♥

JOURNALING THE JOURNEY

♥

♥

♥

♥

JOURNALING THE JOURNEY

♥

JOURNALING THE JOURNEY

♥

♥

♥

♥

♥

JOURNALING THE JOURNEY

♥

♥ (TO BE CONTINUED...)

63554376R00121

Made in the USA
Lexington, KY
10 May 2017